PREACHING
for the
PEOPLE

PREACHING
for the
PEOPLE

LOWELL O. ERDAHL

Abingdon   Nashville

PREACHING FOR THE PEOPLE

Copyright © 1976 by Abingdon

Library of Congress Cataloging in Publication Data

Erdahl, Lowell O.
  Preaching for the people.
  Includes bibliographical references.
  1. Preaching. I. Title.
BV4211.2.E7   251   75-43934

ISBN 0-687-33865-4

Scripture quotations unless otherwise noted are from the Revised Standard Version of the Bible, copyrighted 1946, 1952, and 1971 by the Division of Christian Education, National Council of Churches, and are used by permission.

Scripture quotations noted NEB are from the New English Bible, copyright © the Delegates of the Oxford University Press and the Syndics of the Cambridge University Press, 1961, 1970.

The quotation on pages 25-27 is from *The Teaching Ministry of the Church*, by James D. Smart. Copyright © MCMLIV, by Walter L. Jenkins. Used by permission of The Westminster Press.

The quotations from *The Trouble with the Church* by Helmut Thielicke are abridged from pp. 3, 5, 6 and 21, 63. Translated and Edited by John W. Doberstein. Copyright © 1965 by John W. Doberstein. By permission of Harper & Row, Publishers, Inc.

MANUFACTURED BY THE PARTHENON PRESS AT
NASHVILLE, TENNESSEE, UNITED STATES OF AMERICA

To
CAROL

CONTENTS

PREFACE

There are millions of sermon listeners and thousands of preachers, but few have had extensive experience with preaching from both perspectives. It is especially as a preacher who became a listener that I share some convictions concerning preaching which I hope will be helpful to both clergy and laity.

When, after ten years of parish preaching, I became a professor of homiletics I, in effect, moved from the pulpit to the pew. In each of those teaching years, counting Sunday, chapel, and preaching workshop sermons, I heard nearly as many sermons as I preached in ten years in the parish. Those years in the pew taught me some things about preaching which I never learned in either classroom or pulpit, and part of what follows is therefore presented from the Listener's point of view.

After five years of sermon listening, I returned to the pulpit, and am again wrestling with the specific responsibilities of preparation and proclamation. These concerns are included from the perspective of the Preacher.

The format of this book reflects a continuing dialogue which goes on within me, between myself as listener and myself as preacher. As the Listener, I share what I believe I have a right to expect from preachers. As the Preacher, I reflect upon those expectations and suggest some ways through which I believe they may be fulfilled.

The book is divided into three main sections, each dealing with a question frequently raised by preachers and seminary students: (1) Why should I preach? (2) What should I preach? (3) How should I preach? Through discussion of these questions we will consider an approach to preaching, a message for preaching, and a process of preaching. The volume concludes with Appendix I, giving an example of the steps involved in preparation of a specific sermon, and Appendix II, listing questions for personal reflection and group discussion in congregational as well as seminary and pastoral conference preaching seminars.

CHAPTER ONE

Why Should I Preach?

The Preacher asks, "Why should I preach?"

The Listener replies: "I can only tell why I want you to preach to me. This may seem the beginning of a selfish answer, but am I not justified in believing that your sermons are intended for the benefit of those who hear them? Preaching is for the people! I want you to preach to me and for me.

"But let me be more specific. Knowing two things about me may help to answer your question. I have a yearning and a dream."

A YEARNING

"I yearn for Life—Life with a capital L. I want that Life of which you preachers speak when you tell of 'Life abundant' and 'Life in all its fullness.' Such talk awakens a yearning within me. I yearn for meaning and direction. I look for resources to live from and purposes to live for. I am asking not for the ecstacy of perpetual delight but that my life make sense to me and count for something worthwhile.

"When you preach of faith, remember that I yearn to

11

live with trust and confidence. When you preach about hope, remember that I yearn for hope that dares believe the best is still to be. When you preach of love, remember that I want to be loved and to give myself in love to others.

"I know I don't have enough of faith and hope and love. But, say your worst about me, I do yearn for them. Such yearning sometimes tempts me to have too much faith in the wrong things, too much hope for the wrong things, and too much love for what I should love less. I know my life is distorted by conflicting desires and that I have within me a stubborn perversity resistant to change, but don't let all that overshadow this fact—I do yearn for a life of faith and hope and love.

"This yearning is also awakened by your frequent reference to those qualities the Apostle Paul calls the 'fruit of the Spirit.' When you speak of 'love, joy, peace, patience, kindness, goodness, faithfulness, gentleness, and self-control' (Gal. 5:22-23), something deep within me says 'That's a description of the person I want to be. That's a picture of the life I want to live.' Never mind now that I am far from such life, this fact remains— something within me yearns for those qualities of life. That's the life I want to live. That's the person I want to be."

A DREAM

"Having shared my yearning, I share also the substance of a dream. As I hear you speak of this life

I dare to hope that it is possible for me to live it, not perfectly but much more fully than I am living now.

"My life seems a continuous adventure of possibility fulfillment. Even before I was born my parents sensed both joy and dread as they thought of what I might become. They hoped for a child who would know the joy of health, and they feared for their child the misery of illness.

"Each of our lives is a bundle of unfulfilled possibilities—some positive, some negative; some full of joy, others of pain. Who knows what will be before the day of life is done? Through faulty choice, or tragic circumstances, it is possible that our lives will become a curse to ourselves and to others. Or other possibilities may be fulfilled to bring joy to us and through our lives to others.

"Sensing these possibilities for good and for ill, some can sing "Whatever will be, will be," but I cannot. Life is not programmed from conception to the grave. My choices and those of others affect "whatever will be." When you preach of God's grace, you whet my appetite for life. You awaken a yearning to live more fully and create the dream that this life in grace is possible for me.

"Here then is why I want you to preach to me. Preach to fulfill my yearning and my dream. Preach to give me life of faith and hope and love. Preach to enable me to grow in those 'fruit of the Spirit' qualities. Preach to fulfill in me the possibilities of life in grace."

THE PREACHER REFLECTS ON
THE LISTENER'S REQUEST

As preachers and students of preaching, what do we make of this listener's request? We can reject it for being too selfish or set it aside as an excessive demand beyond any preacher's possibility of fulfillment. Or we can try to understand it in the best light and seek to meet its challenge.

IS ALL SELFISHNESS SINFUL?

Is it sinfully selfish for a listener to ask that we preach to his yearning for life? Do we cater to improper self-interest when we yield to his request? H. Grady Davis warns against preaching which appeals to the listener's self-interest.[1] Such warnings are needed. Many of our selfish desires are sinful, and it would be wrong to cater to them. But is every aspect of selfish desire sinful? Is it wrong for a hungry person to wish for food or a thirsty person for water? Is it sinful for the sick to desire health and the lonely to wish for companionship? Is it wicked to desire sexual fulfillment or to yearn for an increase in faith, hope, and love? A prayer for personal growth in the fruit of the Spirit is selfish; is it also sinful?

All desire can be corrupted by perverse pride, but every desire is not sinful in itself. Some yearnings are part of a God-given hunger for life and are in themselves as sacred as their perversions are sinful. We see the perversions in ourselves and in others. Inordinate hunger for food leads to gluttony, inordinate or misdirected hunger for sexual fulfillment to lust, inordinate hunger for spiritual perfection to self-righteousness. If our only motive is to excel others in virtue, it may be sinful to pray for an increase in faith, hope, and love. Pride transforms our God-given yearning for life into the self-saving lust for life of which Jesus spoke when he said, "Whoever would save his life will lose it" (Luke 9:24). Our desire for life may be so possessive that, like a child who greedily hugs his pet rabbit to death in an effort to keep it for himself, we kill the very life we seek.

Our desires can be and to some extent are always perverted by our pride, but in all these experiences we can see behind the sinfulness a holy desire for life. With F. W. Robertson we seek to see "the soul of goodness in things evil."[2] Deep within the playboy who lives by self-indulgence and the pietist who lives by self-righteousness is a common God-given yearning for life. Show me any person in whatever state of sinfulness, and I still wager that deep within that person is a holy desire for that life which throbs with faith and hope and love.

Many people, deeply hurt, retreat into despair. To protect themselves from further disappointment they cease to hope for anything. Some, overwhelmed by pain of mind or body, choose death as an escape from the only life they know. But in these situations too, I still wager on the presence of a deep, if hidden, yearning for life. Suicide does not prove the absence of such yearning. It rather reveals that for this person there seemed no possibility of experiencing life in fullness.

CREATED FOR CHRIST

Colossians says of Christ, "All things were created . . . for him" (1:16). Does that mean that we are created to live the life Christ invites us to live? Are we most fully human when we live in him and subhuman apart from him? Is it natural to be "in Christ" and unnatural to be "out of Christ"? Is E. Stanley Jones correct when he says, "The Christian way is the natural way—the way we are made to live. Everything else is unnatural"? [3] To me the answer to each of these questions is an emphatic yes!

This does not mean that we are created to live under the burdens various forms of Christianity impose upon life; it does mean that in Christ the true way of life is revealed to us and made possible for us. When Jesus said, "Whoever would save his life will lose it; and whoever loses his life for my sake, he will save it" (Luke 9:24), he stated a fact of life. According to that statement, there are two basically different styles or ways of living. One is self-saving, the other self-losing. Jesus lived the self-losing way. He gave himself away in trust and yielding to God, his Father, and he gave himself away in love and service to people who needed him. Jesus' life was an adventure of continuous abandonment to God in trust and to people in love. We look back upon that life as the most fully human this world has known.

Jesus reveals the life we are created to live. When he calls us to follow him he invites us back to ourselves and into the fullness of what it is to be human. We are created for abandonment! We are created to give ourselves away! We are created for the self-losing life! "The entire way of life for the man of Christ," said Luther, consists in just two things: "Faith and love. . . . Faith receives, loves gives."[4] Jesus says, in effect, that the true way of life *for the human person* consists in trust in God and love of neighbor. The call of Jesus is an invitation to give ourselves away in the double abandonment of self-giving trust to God and self-forgetful caring for others. This is the life for which we most deeply yearn. We therefore join F. W. Robertson in saying, "Let us comprehend our own nature, ourselves and our destinies. God is our rest, the only one who can quench the fever of our desire. God in Christ is what we want."[5] Such is the holy desire God has put within us. We want Christ and the life God gives in him.

MY AIM IN PREACHING

Therefore as a preacher I will affirm my listener's yearning for life. I will intentionally seek to identify my message with his God-given self-interest. I will make it my purpose to give him life.

The disciples were commissioned to declare "all the words of this Life" (Acts 5:20). (The RSV prints that Life with a capital L.) I take those words as my commission for preaching. I will seek in every way I

can to share this life in all its fullness. My aim in
preaching will be to enable my listener to live this life,
to make it possible for him to live in the trust and love
of the adventure of abandonment to which Christ calls
us. I will heed Paul Scherer's suggestion: "When you
look into the faces of your congregation, leave your
disappointments at home, and turn your imagination
loose in this amazing world. Speak to their other and
better selves." [6] My goal in the pulpit will be to help my
hearers become more fully human—to be more nearly
the persons they were born to be and to live more
nearly this life they were created to live.

PREACH TO THE POSSIBILITIES OF PEOPLE!

I will, therefore, see my hearers not as problems but
as possibilities. Problem-solution sermons can be a
helpful means of sharing new life. Harry Emerson
Fosdick deserves credit for personalizing preaching
through a problem-solution approach.

> People come to church on Sunday with every kind of
> personal difficulty and problem the flesh is heir to. . . . That
> was the place to start—with the real problems of the people.
> . . . Every sermon should have for its main business the
> head on constructive meeting of some problem which was
> puzzling minds, burdening consciences, distracting lives. [7]

But, as Fosdick was also aware, people are not just
problems. They are possibilities waiting for fulfillment.
If we forget that fact we may become so preoccupied

with problems that our problem-centered preaching creates more problems than it solves.

Preaching to the possibilities of people involves more than belief in native human ability. Confidence in the positive potential of people is founded on trust in the graceful presence of God. Self-centered, "possibility" thinking may give a temporary lift to life, but if it is only telling ourselves or others "You can do it," we are inviting disillusionment and despair.

With so much negative, impossibility thinking in the world we may need the corrective of Norman Vincent Peale's positive thinking and Robert Schuller's possibility thinking, but we need beware of any emphasis which may lead to a cult of auto-suggestion and self-assertion which easily becomes a substitute for true life in grace.[8] While gratefully affirming all human gifts, the emphasis of our message centers on God's mercy and power and not on our goodness or ability. Grace alone opens the way to new life and enables us to preach to the possibilities of people.

THE POSSIBILITIES OF PREACHING

Yet we may wonder, is it really possible for us to help fulfill these possibilities through preaching?

Our answer may depend more on our experience as listeners than as preachers. If we have heard at least one sermon through which we ourselves received some measure of new life in grace, we will agree it can happen. Beyond such personal experience we remember the testimony of others across twenty centuries

who testify that some preaching has been a means of
grace for them. Recalling what preaching has meant to
others helps enable us to believe it is possible for our
preaching to be life-giving.

As a preacher I will, therefore, think and act in terms
of the possibilities of preaching. Preaching too, will be
not a problem to be solved but a positive possibility to
be fulfilled. I will approach the task with confidence
that God can use my sermons as he has used the
preaching of others.

CHAPTER TWO

What Should I Preach?

The Preacher asks, "What should I preach?"

The Listener replies: "There is a message I need to hear you preach to me. You may again be fearful of such a subjective answer, thinking that I will tell you what I *want*, but not what I *need* to hear. To allay such fear, I assure you that many meaningful sermons have been among those I enjoyed the least. I don't need to be coddled, and in my most sensible moments I don't want such preaching. I need and want a message which can begin to fulfill in me some of those positive possibilities of life in grace. After hearing hundreds of sermons I believe that I can tell you some things about the message creative of such life.

"I need preaching which proclaims three words, and each not just a word from the preacher but a Word from the Lord. These are God's *yes!* God's *no!* and God's *go!*"

GOD'S YES!

"To live new life I need to hear a great yes affirming the presence and pardon and power of God. I need to be reassured again and again that God loves me and that his gracious mercy and power over-abound my sin and weakness. I cannot talk myself into having faith or obtain hope by screwing up my courage; nor do I become a more loving person by deciding to be so. Therefore don't just tell me to decide to be a better person or even to decide for Christ. Proclaim God's yes to me. Affirm the grace which makes faith, hope, and love possible.

"Do you want me to have the faith for which I yearn? Then do more than tell me to have faith. Proclaim God's yes to create faith. Answer the often secret questions of my heart: Does God love me and those I love? Is his forgiveness big enough to cover things of which I am most ashamed? Is there power present to heal and lift my broken life? When death draws near to me and to those I love, are there power-backed promises that can give hope for life beyond the living of these days? Is there any specific good news for me in my peculiarities, my loneliness, my fears, my weakness, my doubt? Can this world be a better place because I've lived in it? Such are a few of the wonderings of my heart, and you preachers have let me dare believe that God's answer in Jesus Christ to each of these questions is a grace-filled yes. Let me hear that yes over and over again. That yes is food for faith. That yes has given me a taste of new life. Let that yes be front and center in your preaching, and let nothing said on other themes deny or dilute it. Apart from God's yes there is no hope for me at all. What should you preach? Declare to me the yes of God in Jesus Christ."

GOD'S NO!

"As I plead to hear that great yes, I am aware that I also need God's no to knock the props out from under my idolatrous confidence in myself and the things I call mine. I need to hear that no which stands over against my sinful pride and pretense. When I live in self-complacent conceit and with contempt for others, when I've settled down in self-satisfaction, I need to hear that no which exposes the folly and hurtfulness of my manner of life. I need a no which breaks through my defenses and reveals my need of grace.

"I am not asking to be scolded or told off. There may be a streak of masochism in me that takes satisfaction in a verbal lashing, but the no I seek is a word not of punishment but of confrontation. Don't just give me forty lashes for my sins—confront me with my sins and my sinfulness. Show me myself as I am in my folly and perversity as well as in my wisdom and strength. Speak a clear no to every aspect of my life, personal and social, which stands contrary to the way of Christ. Expose me to myself that I may see the condition and consequences of my life.

"Be both kind and honest. Be kind enough to tell me the truth. Deal with me as firmly as with an alcoholic. Speak with the frankness of one who cares enough to risk the truth. Don't let me go on living in a world of self-deception and make-believe. Don't let me settle for the complacency of any fool's paradise. What should you preach? Speak God's no to all in me which appears contrary to the way of Christ."

GOD'S GO!

"As you speak that yes to save and sustain me and that no to convict and correct me, also speak God's go, sending me to the work I've been created to do. Lead me into a deeper sense of responsibility toward God, toward other people, and toward all creation. Speak this go in relation to all of the dimensions of my life—personal, corporate, political, financial and the rest. Express the go through a 'show.' Show me the possibilities for sharing and service which call for my concern and action. Remind me of the need for justice as well as charity. Expand my circle of responsibility beyond self and family to others whose lives might be lifted through my words and deeds.

"I'm not asking you to dictate how I should spend my time and my money. But I want you to help me make these decisions in the light of Christ's great commission. While something in me would like to forget that altogether, something else calls me toward a more responsible life. I look to your sermons to help me face and fulfill these responsibilities.

"This, then, is one listener's answer to your question, What Shall I Preach? Preach God's Yes! God's No! and God's Go!"

THE PREACHER REFLECTS ON
THE LISTENER'S REQUEST

As a preacher I hear the Listener asking for proclamation of both the gospel and the law, and for direction in

Christian living. His request leads to consideration of two distinctions preachers and hearers need to keep in mind: the distinction between preaching and teaching; and the distinction between the gospel and the law.

THE DISTINCTION BETWEEN
PREACHING AND TEACHING

Preaching and teaching belong together, but they are not identical. Preaching is the proclamation of the gospel and the law to effect the initial and continuous conversion of persons from life centered in self to life centered in grace. Teaching is instruction to deepen our understanding and guide our living. Preaching aims to bring us into and to keep us in Christ. Teaching aims to guide us in understanding and living the life we have in Christ.

James Smart believes misunderstanding has resulted, in this regard, from uncritical acceptance of C. H. Dodd's expression of the difference between *Kerygma* and *didache*.[1] Smart's statement of the proper distinction is worth pondering at length.

The content of preaching and of teaching is the same. But preaching essentially is the proclamation of this Word of God *to man in his unbelief*. Both outside and inside the Church that definition proves adequate. Preaching is the call to men in their sin and unbelief to repent and receive the good news that God is ready to come to them, and that, by the power of his Word and his Spirit dwelling in them, he will establish them in the glad free life of his Kingdom. We need the preaching of the word as Christians, because, no matter how far we have gone in faith, there still remains a root of sin and unbelief in us, a place in each of us into which the humbling, transforming word of the gospel has not yet come. The preacher who makes the mistake of thinking that the good Christians sitting in the pews before him no longer need to hear the call to repentance or the proclamation of the nearness of the Kingdom in Christ has lost all understanding both of the gospel itself and of the natures of those to whom he is commissioned to proclaim it. Preaching addresses itself always to man in the distress of his separation from and rebellion against God.

What, then, is teaching? Teaching essentially (but not exclusively) addresses itself to the situation of the man who has repented and turned to God and to the situation of children of believers who through the influence of their parents have in them a measure of faith, even though they have also in them a large measure of unbelief. . . .

The distinction between preaching and teaching must be maintained, but it must not be allowed to become a false and un-Biblical distinction. When the Church exalts teaching at the expense of preaching, it inevitably becomes moralistic and legalistic. This can be seen in rabbinic Judaism and also in wide areas of present-day Protestantism. People are assumed to need only teaching. The rock of unbelief and sin in them is forgotten. A gospel that calls men to repent and believe, sending them down into the death of their old self in repentance that they may rise into the new life of faith, seems out of place. Salvation becomes a quite simple matter of having the right ideals and measuring up to them as well as we can. Teaching, without a kerygmatic preaching alongside it to remind it of the common origin and common task of both, can very easily become a total falsification of Christianity.

Equally unfortunate are the results when the ministry confines its attention to the kerygma, the proclamation of the gospel, and ignores the task of teaching. Such a ministry fails because it refuses to follow the Word that is preached into the lives of the hearers and to take seriously the problems that the believer begins at once to meet in his response to the gospel and in his personal growth in the knowledge of God.[2]

When the Listener requests God's yes, no, and go, he asks for both *preaching* of gospel and law, and for *teaching* which clarifies the meaning of the gospel and the law and which gives direction for living.

THE DISTINCTION BETWEEN THE GOSPEL AND THE LAW

Luther maintained that the true test of a theologian is in the ability to distinguish between the law and the gospel. The Listener's request for a clear yes and no prompts us to seek such a distinction. Like preaching and teaching, the gospel and the law belong together but are not identical.

THE GOSPEL

The gospel is God's great yes in Jesus Christ. "Our word to you," says Paul, "has not been Yes and No. . . . In him it is always Yes. For all promises of God find their Yes in him" (II Cor. 1:18-20). The gospel speaks for God saying "I love you" to every person. The gospel declares, as Luther liked to say, that God loves each of us even more than we love ourselves. It proclaims that we cannot even get God to stop loving us. God loves as the sun shines, whether we like it or not. God loves us, not because we are good—nor does he stop loving us because we are bad; God loves because "God is love" (I John 4:8, 16).

This love is merciful, accepting and receiving us as we are. Dr. George Aus, of Luther Theological Seminary, stressed during my student days that "just as we shouldn't be so proud as to think that we have no sins, so also we shouldn't be so proud as to think that our sins are too big for God to forgive." God's gracious mercy over-abounds our abounding sin, and, whatever our feelings may tell us, the gospel declares that God loves us now and will love us forever.

God's love is mighty as well as merciful. Grace is power as well as pardon. This power is our strength in weakness and our hope in death. By God's power we live and work all our days. By *his* power we rise and "walk in newness of life" (Rom. 6:4). By *his* power we are not only forgiven in our sins but cleansed from our sins. By *his* power the fruit of the Spirit grows within us. By *his* power healing spreads through us and from us. By *his* power we die in the hope of new life beyond our dying. All this is by God's grace alone. Through it all there is not one thing of which we can proudly boast. All we can do is give thanks to God!

BY GRACE THROUGH FAITH

We cannot even take credit for our faith. We are not justified by, or on account of, our faith but "by grace . . . through faith" (Eph. 2:8). Fosdick stressed that faith is created by that in which we have faith. If I trust you, it is because you have made it possible for me to do so.

Your trustworthiness has created my trust in you. So also with faith in God. Faith, said Luther, is "born of the gospel." The promises of God's gracious mercy and power create our faith. We do not trust by trying. We begin to trust when we quit trying. And we quit trying when the gospel promises lure our attention away from ourselves to the pardon and power of God. Charles Spurgeon tells that the turning point of his life came when a preacher lifted up Christ and invited him to look away from himself to Christ and to God's promises in him. Spurgeon could later speak of himself as having been "saved by looking."[3]

Luther saw faith to be pure passivity. Having faith is an act of becoming and being passive. When we have faith we do nothing but let God do all that he has promised to do. Our struggling and striving may be used of God to bring us to faith, but faith is not produced by striving. "Faith comes from what is heard, and what is heard comes by the preaching of Christ" (Rom. 10:17). Paul Tillich describes this experience as being "struck by grace."

> We cannot transform our lives, unless we allow them to be transformed by that stroke of grace. It happens; or it does not happen. And certainly it does not happen if we try to force it upon ourselves, just as it shall not happen so long as we think, in our self-complacency, that we have no need of it.[4]

GOD'S GIFTS AND OUR FREEDOM

We deal here with profound matters touching upon the sovereignty of God and human freedom. I do not

claim fully to fathom this mystery but believe that
Luther, in the Small Catechism, is true to scripture and
experience when he says, "I believe that I cannot by my
own understanding or effort believe in Jesus Christ my
Lord, or come to him," and that his only hope is that
"the Holy Spirit has called me through the gospel." As
the new light of grace dawned upon him, Luther saw
that salvation is a gift and that we have no freedom to
give gifts to ourselves. Gifts can only be received from
those who give them. We cannot by fervent willing or
determined trying give them to ourselves.

Gifts can be received but not achieved. We may
destroy a gift, but we cannot create it. Life is a gift
which we have freedom to abuse or to destroy, but we
have no freedom to give it to ourselves. Sight is a gift.
Sighted, we can will to become blind; but if we are
blind we cannot by striving give ourselves the gift of
sight. Sleep is a gift. When we try to sleep we remain
awake. When we think of other things the gift of sleep
comes of itself. Self-centered trying drives the gift
away; self-forgetful trusting lets the gift come.

In our self-centered trying we are often like a child
frantically chasing the butterflies. All efforts result in
failure. Giving up, he kneels in the grass to rest and
soon a butterfly comes to land on his shoulder.

Why these examples? To underscore this basic fact:
"For *by grace* you have been saved *through faith;* and
this is not your own doing, it is *the gift* of God—not
because of works, lest any man should boast" (Eph.
2:8-9; emphasis added). That fact speaks of the limits of

our ability. We have no power in ourselves to will or win God's gifts for ourselves. Efforts to do so are futile attempts to save ourselves. Such trying is evidence that we are still relying upon ourselves rather than trusting in God. We do not become less self-centered by trying to be so. Self-forgetfulness begins when something or someone outside of ourselves draws our attention away from ourselves.

When we quit trying and start looking to God's promises in Christ we begin to live by grace. Jesus lures us out of self-centered trying and into self-forgetful faith. He calls us away from efforts to achieve, and into trust which receives the gifts he offers.

THE LANGUAGE OF THE GOSPEL

If those who hear our sermons are to come to faith and to grow in faith, we must do other than exhort them to "try to have faith" or "will to believe" or "decide for Christ." Following the guidance of C. F. W. Walther, we will not make "an appeal to believe in a manner as if a person could make himself believe or at least help toward that end" but will rather seek to "preach faith into a person's heart by laying the gospel promises before him." [5]

Our task is not to persuade people to decide for Christ but to lift up Christ so that he may draw them to himself. We are witnesses to Christ more than lawyers for Christ. "Concerning the language of preaching," said Paul Scherer, "we should do better perhaps to borrow not from the courts but from courtship." [6] We

are to woo more than to persuade. Gerhard Forde puts it
well when he says:

Instances in everyday life give us a kind of picture of
what is involved here. Whenever we have to do with things
that affect us most deeply and really change the course of
our lives we begin to speak a somewhat different kind of
language. We talk of "being moved" by some profound
experience, perhaps by great art or music, or we talk of
"being inspired" by someone or something. Precisely at
those points we no longer speak of language of deliberation
and choice. We are "moved," "inspired" by something
from without. Something outside or "above us" gets at us
and changes us. In more contemporary language we talk of
being "turned on." Perhaps an even better illustration is
that of love. When love really comes to us we often begin
speaking that strange language. We speak of it not as
something we choose, but as something we "fall into." Or
we even begin to say sometimes "It must be fate," or "that
marriage was made in heaven" or "written in the stars"
and so on. Granted, these are perhaps rather pagan
expressions. But they mirror that strange new language we
begin to speak when we are truly grasped by something
that was somehow "above" us, something we could not
produce on our own. In love, we are not even afraid of
"fate." We are not afraid of being caught up, transformed,
having the whole world made new for us. Luther wanted to
insist that something like this happens in an even more
profound sense when you really hear the gospel. You are
"inspired" by the Spirit that is Holy, you are reached by
that which was out of reach, you are made new! [7]

CHRISTIAN LIFE—PASSIVE AND ACTIVE

Stress on faith as pure passivity and on the importance of "letting God do what he has promised" may

seem an escape from responsibility. "Let God do it" may sound like "Let George do it," and that can be a cop-out. But not necessarily. If I need open-heart surgery and George is the heart surgeon, I had better let George do it. Through being passive to George's action, I hope I will be enabled to become more usefully active than was possible before. So also if God is God and I am a creature, sinful, weak, one day to die, I had better let God do it. As I let him do his work, I'm set free to my work. In passivity toward God, I am liberated for activity toward people.

In living the Christian life, passivity and activity go together. We again recall Luther's assertion that the whole way of life for the Christian person consists in faith in God and love of neighbor. Faith is passive, love is active. As we rest in the grace of God, we work serving people. Our dual life of rest and work is illustrated by an ocean liner. While passively at rest upon the sea, its engines are actively at work to carry passengers to their destination.

Or in more personal terms our passive trust and active love are illustrated by the lifeguard who rests in the water even as he works to reach and rescue a drowning person. I learned to swim as an adult and can vividly remember the day I discovered that the water was my friend, eager to hold me up, and not, as previously feared, my enemy trying to pull me down. The dependability of the friendly water led me from fear to faith. When I began trusting the water to hold me up I began to swim. Then the joy of swimming began, and only then could I consider the possibility of becoming a lifeguard. Only through passive trust was the possibility of active lifesaving open to me.

So also in Christian life. At rest upon the grace of God we are freed from the frantic and futile work of holding ourselves up. The grace of God calls us into a continuous adventure of abandonment, inviting us in every moment to let go of ourselves and of all to which we cling and to rest upon God's promised presence. These promises lure us even to let go of God. Assured of his promises in Christ we need not try to feverishly cling to him but can let go and rest in his grace trusting that he holds us with love that will not let us go. In the security of that love we are free to forget ourselves and care for others. Lifted and held in God's grace we need waste no effort on lifting ourselves but can concentrate on lifting the lives of others. Passive in trust we are freed to be active in love.

THE LAW

When the Listener requests God's no as well as God's yes, he is asking for the law as well as the gospel. Like Karl Barth, he puts the gospel first, reminding us that the law is a form of the gospel.[8] God's no, like God's yes, is an expression of his love. Because God says yes to life, he must say no to all in us and around us that is anti-life.

WHAT THE LAW DOES

The Listener rejects "law-preaching" which is only sermonic scolding or moralistic tongue-lashing. We can be scolded without hearing the law, and we can hear the law without feeling scolded. True hearing of the law does more than make us feel guilty. It may do that, but it always does something more. The law makes us aware not only of our sinfulness but also of our inability to do anything significant to remedy our situation.

The purpose of law is not to punish us. God takes no delight in watching us suffer. The law confronts us with the reality of our predicament. It reveals our weakness and finitude as well as our sin. The law does not whip us, it rather knocks the props from under our .idols.

Properly heard, the law does not induce us to try harder. It may temporarily have that effect, but the purpose of the law is to bring home the fact that in relation to our attempts to win a place with God, there is no use in trying at all. The law kills our lively notions of omnipotence, silences our excuses and alibis, and brings us face to face with ourselves as we are. It does not *impose* rules upon us, but *exposes* what we are at heart. Preaching *of* the law is therefore the constant context of *teaching from* the law. First the confrontation, then correction and guidance.

This may seem negative and self-deprecating but the real negativity is in our negation of the reality concerning ourselves. True self-deprecation is in our pretending to be other than we are. It is certainly humiliating for us proud mortals to admit our failures and finitude, but such an admission does not make us less human. We begin to be truly human when we abandon our pretense to be divine. Christ's call to die *to* self is not a call to death *of* self. Death *to* self as "god" is birth *of* self as human being.

FORMS OF THE LAW

As an example, think of the experience of an alcoholic. The gospel for an alcoholic is the promise of new life given by a power greater than oneself. The law is *everything* that brings inner realization of both his sickness and his helplessness to overcome it. As long as he thinks that he can control his drinking, the law has not completed its work. The law says a constant no to every form of his self-saving effort, and only when those efforts cease and the alcoholic takes the first step of the A. A. program—admitting to being powerless over alcohol—has he really heard the law's clear voice. To maintain sobriety he lives in daily awareness of that voice and can never return to the notion that "I can control it on my own."

The alcoholic's situation pictures what is true of each of us. We all live with a condition of sinfulness and finitude which we are powerless to overcome. The gospel is God's offer in Christ of a power beyond ourselves which can give us new life. The law is *everything* that brings realization of our need. Confrontation by the law is not confined to specifically Christian or even religious experiences. Anything that helps us face our sin and weakness is the work of the law. Non-Christian, nonreligious persons may be already so overwhelmed by failure and finitude that their need is not more law but much gospel.

WE WHO ARE RELIGIOUS NEED THE LAW

We professionally religious people may need more law than the irreligious, who may enter the kingdom before us. Our religiosity may be a substitute for, rather than a sign of, life in grace. Even while repeating the publican's prayer, "God, be merciful to me a sinner," we may be inwardly praying with the Pharisee, "God, I thank thee that I am not like other men." We sense some need of mercy and power but do not see ourselves as totally dependent upon grace as are flagrant sinners.

But "God doesn't help us save ourselves." [9] As long as we think we can get by on our own, with a little help from our friendly Father, we are still in need of being confronted into self-awareness. If we are living with such self-deception, the Scottish pastor J. W. Stevenson may, through his shared experience, help us see ourselves as we are.

> One night, when I had gone up the glen to a shepherd's cottage, I found him sitting at his fireside with his daughter opposite him, unable to raise his eyes towards her for anger. He was ashamed of what had happened; but it was not shame only. He was holding on to some idea of right and wrong, because it was what he had lived by; and now it was keeping him apart from this girl when they needed each other most. He wanted to get up and put his arm around her shoulders as she sat there, bent over the fire; but something else in him made him determined not to do it. He was struggling against himself. . . .

He was on the edge of breaking down. That was his hope. He had to break down. The woman in adultery was once more before the Pharisee. This is our human predicament; this is the confusion we are in, that we can scarcely judge evil without increasing the evil in ourselves.

This is the key to the nature of our sin—why Christ has to break in, why He has to break down what is shutting us off from God and Man.

I was afraid for this man, as he began to lose grip on himself—until I saw that it was his grip on himself which held him back from God and from what God wanted him to be.

I was on the instant ready to comfort him and bring him back to himself—until I saw that this was exactly where he must not be brought back. The evil was not in the crumbling of his life but in the shoring of it up. . . .

Our fears are for the wrong things—fear that our defenses will fall down, when it is our defenses which put us in peril; fear that we may have to be changed, when our wretchedness comes from going on as we are.[10]

This destruction of our defenses is the work of the law, and it can be a terrifying experience, especially in the absence of the gospel. The law, as Luther said, is meant to drive us to Christ, but apart from the gospel it can drive us to despair. We therefore preach the law in the context of the gospel. Confrontation with the alcoholic's powerlessness is presented in the context of power greater than oneself. Confrontation with our pride and powerlessness needs also to be kept in the context of Christ's pardon and power. Our hope in God frees us to face our helplessness. Weak in ourselves, we find strength in him.

Lest this talk of weakness be taken as an expression

of human worthlessness and incapacity for service we stress that when we surrender our lives to God's pardon and power we surrender to no other. We bow before God as creatures in need of grace, but we stand tall in the presence of the enemies of life, ready to do battle, empowered with all the strength God supplies. Pretending to be gods, we are weak; as human beings used of God we can be strong in his power and for his service.

Our job as preachers is to reveal both the open door to new life in Christ and the closed doors of life apart from Christ. As we affirm God's yes to life, we also proclaim God's no to all that is anti-life.

THOUGHTS TO PONDER AND DEBATE

To encourage wrestling with the distinction between the gospel and the law, the following statements are included for reflection and debate.

  I. On the Preaching of the Gospel

    A. The preaching of the gospel does not tell me what to do to be saved. It tells me that I do not need to do anything to be saved.

    B. The preaching of the gospel does not demand a response of faith. It creates a response of faith.

    C. The preaching of the gospel does not demand anything. It is not a demand but an offer.

    D. The preaching of the gospel does not command me to be active for God. It invites me to be passive toward God and to let God act.

E. The preaching of the gospel is not just to convert pagans into Christians. It is also to reconvert the pagan in Christians.

F. The preaching of the gospel does not demand that I decide for Christ. It invites me to live in the decision God in Christ has made for me.

G. The preaching of the gospel does not tell me that God will love me if I repent and have faith. It tells me that I can repent and have faith because God loves me.

H. The preaching of the gospel is always necessary. Whatever else I need, including the law, I also need assurance of God's love.

I. The preaching of the gospel frees me from the job of earning God's love and frees me for the job of loving my neighbor.

J. The preaching of the gospel does not offer grace on certain conditions to be met. Grace is received when I quit trying to meet conditions and start trusting God's promises.

K. The preaching of the gospel does not just lead me into self-examination or self-assertion. It leads me out of myself into self-forgetfulness and self-surrender.

L. The preaching of the gospel does not cause me to look more at myself. It directs my attention to Christ and frees me to see my neighbor.

M. The preaching of the gospel does not persuade me to make up my mind. It woos me to give up my heart.

N. The preaching of the gospel does not tell me what to do to get God to love me. It tells me that there is nothing I can do to get God to stop loving me.

O. The preaching of the gospel does not tell me to quit sinning so that God will forgive me. It tells me not to be so proud as to think my sins are too big for God to forgive.

P. The preaching of the gospel does not tell me to change to get God to accept me. It tells me that God accepts me as I am.

II. On the Preaching of the Law

A. The preaching of the law does not scold. It confronts my idols, especially the god of self.

B. The preaching of the law does not impose morality on me. It exposes the immorality and mortality within me.

C. The preaching of the law does more than reveal that I am sinful. It also reveals my inability to be anything else.

D. The preaching of the law not only reveals that I am a sinful creature, it confronts me with the sin and stupidity of playing creator.

E. The preaching of the law is not talking about the law. It is thrusting a sword through the proud pretender within me.

F. The preaching of the law does not make me try harder. It reveals the futility of my trying at all.

G. The preaching of the law does not strengthen

my defenses. It breaks them down and exposes
my need of grace.

H. The preaching of the law does not show the
way from me to God. It declares that there is
no way from me to God.

I. The preaching of the law does not happen
only in the pulpit. It happens whenever and
wherever and however my sinfulness, weakness, and finitude are revealed to me.

J. The preaching of the law is not always
necessary. There is no need to kill the dead;
they need to be raised to life.

K. The preaching of the law does not contradict
the gospel. We preach the law in the context of
the gospel.

L. The preaching of the law is not just for the
pagan non-Christian. It is also for the non-
Christian pagan within all Christians.

M. The preaching of the law does not exclude
teaching *from* the law, but teaching *from* the
law can wrongly replace preaching *of* the law.

N. The preaching of the law is not to condemn
but to convict and to correct. Persons in Christ
are free from the condemnation of the law but
no one is free from the law's conviction and
correction.

DIRECTION FOR DAILY LIVING

In addition to the yes and no of gospel and law, the
Listener asks for the go of the great commission. E.

Stanley Jones may be responsible for popularizing the expression "Let go and let God." The proclamation of the gospel and law is directed toward that kind of letting go and letting God. But Christian life involves more than inner surrender to God; it also includes outer service to people. Therefore, Jones suggests that the more complete picture of life in Christ is "Let go, Let God," and then "Let's go." He says, in effect, "Now let's go to work living out this new life in Christ through active work and witness."

THEREFORE!

The teaching aspect of preaching seeks to shed light on the specific opportunities and responsibilities involved in Christ's commission to go. It is illustrated by the ethical sections of Paul's letters which spell out practical implications of the message of God's mercy and judgment. These sections begin with an implied or stated *therefore*. "I appeal to you *therefore*, brethren, . . . do not be conformed to this world but be transformed by the renewal of your mind" (Rom. 12:1). Or having proclaimed the promise of resurrection: "*Therefore*, my beloved brethren, be steadfast, immovable, always abounding in the work of the Lord, knowing that in the Lord your labor is not in vain" (I Cor. 15:58). Far from seeing the resurrection promises as reason to give up on this life, Paul, because of them, sees every day and deed as having eternal significance.

The central *therefore* of the Christian life is implied

in verses such as "A new commandment I give to you,
that you love one another; even as I have loved you,
that you also love one another" (John 13:34) and "In
this is love, not that we loved God but that he loved us
and sent his Son to be the expiation for our sins.
Beloved, if God so loved us, we also ought to love one
another. . . . We love, because he first loved us!" (I John
4:10-11, 19). These verses say, in effect, you are loved,
therefore love. Being loved not only obligates but also
enables us to love. The promises of grace open the
possibilities of graceful loving. John Cobb writes
insightfully of how gracious love opens the way to
genuine loving.

> Love is, . . . on the one hand, the only salvation of the
> spiritual man and, on the other hand, unattainable by his
> own efforts. The spiritual man can only love when he is
> freed from the necessity to love, that is, when he knows
> himself already loved in his self-preoccupation. Only if
> man finds that he is already accepted in his sin and
> sickness, can he accept his own self-preoccupation as it is;
> and only then can his psychic economy be opened toward
> others, to accept them as they are—not in order to save
> himself, but because he doesn't need to save himself. We
> love only because we are first loved. In this way, and only
> in this way, can the spiritual man genuinely and purely
> love.[11]

The no of the law exposes our lovelessness and the
lie that genuine love is attainable by our own efforts.
The yes of the gospel assures that we are loved in our
self-preoccupation and thereby frees us to go in
self-forgetful caring for others.

SHOW ME THE POSSIBILITIES

The Listener asks that we express the go through a show—"show me the possibilities for sharing and service that call for my concern and action." This is a dangerous request. With Paul, we must often acknowledge that we have no direct word from the Lord, but we still seek to set the specific issues of life within the light of the biblical witness as we understand it.

Earnest Christians wrestle daily with decisions concerning how to spend time and money. They wonder how to be better wives, husbands, parents, and children, and how to be more responsible citizens of community, country, and world. Issues related to war, waste of resources, hunger, poverty, pollution, excessive population, and the like are vital for all of us. Can we continue our present pattern of consumption? What about abortion and euthanasia? How do we relate to people of different races, religions, and life-styles? What do we make of all the liberation movements— black, youth, gay, women's, and the rest? These questions compel our attention and action, and none is automatically answered by affirming the American way of life or by saying a prayer or quoting a Bible verse.

No wise preacher will attempt a series of sermons giving the last word on each of these issues, but in the course of our preaching we will seek to let the light of Christ fall upon these concerns to enable Christian attitudes and behavior. As we do so we will encourage shared reflection so that Christian witness may be revealed through the people of Christ as well as through the preacher.

THE LISTENER REACTS TO THE PREACHER

A SERMON OR A LECTURE?

"It is clear that you intend to proclaim the gospel and the law, but there are times when I believe you fail to accomplish your purpose.

"You sometimes talk *about* the gospel without proclaiming the gospel. I fail to hear God's yes. What I hear is a religious-sounding lecture, a kind of oral theological essay. It then seems you think that what I need to be a Christian is to agree with your ideas—as if *believing the idea* that 'justification is by grace through faith' were the same as *being* justified by grace through faith. Having faith in God is not the same as holding an idea about God. A lecture about food is not a steak dinner. Nor is a lecture about the gospel the same as a proclamation of the gospel.

"I am not against some 'lecturish' elements within sermons. You are correct that I want teaching as well as preaching, but I don't want lectures instead of sermons. When I'm hungry I want a meal and not a menu or a page from a cookbook. A sermon may be similar to a dinner at some gourmet restaurants. The waitress tells about the food while serving it. She teaches us and feeds us at the same time. Your most meaningful sermons seem like that. They are food for our lives. You offer Christ as the Bread of Life but at the same time give instruction and explanation along the way.

"To illustrate further, there is a difference between a lecture on 'God is Love' and a sermon which says 'God loves you!' The lecture is a discussion about God, the sermon is a personal word from God. A lecture seeks to explain something, a sermon seeks to share a life-changing message. We listeners will attempt to translate a lecture *about* God into a word *from* God, but your sermons are best when such translation is unnecessary. Let us hear that yes from God in direct personal terms. Let your sermons be more than lectures about grace. Let them be means of grace into our lives.

"So also with what you call preaching the law. Your sermons are sometimes general discussions of 'the sinfulness of man' which don't reach me on the inside. They don't topple my idols. I need personal confrontation, and you sometimes give it. There are times when I see myself in your illustrations and feel as David must have felt when Nathan said, "You are the man" (II Sam. 12:7). I don't always like that; but I know I need it, and I'm grateful for it."

THE PREACHER RESPONDS TO THE LISTENER'S REACTION

THE DIFFERENCE BETWEEN SERMON AND LECTURE

"Your reaction tempts me to be defensive. I agree that there is a difference between a sermon and a lecture. Fosdick put the distinction in terms similar to yours. 'A lecture is chiefly concerned with a *subject* to be elucidated; a sermon is chiefly concerned with an *object* to be achieved.'[12] The purpose of a lecture is to explain a subject. The purpose of a sermon is to transform a life. But granting that, isn't it true that explaining subjects is one way of transforming lives? Perhaps that is what you mean by asking for sermons that combine proclamation and explanation. John Wesley's *Journal* reports his having gone to certain places where 'I proclaimed the love of Christ to sinners' or 'Offered "the grace of our Lord Jesus Christ."'[13] I hope my sermons, too, offer Christ and are means of grace rather than being just lectures *about* Christ and *about* grace."

A GRACE-EVENT

"I am also distressed to hear that my sermons sometimes give the impression that a Christian is one who holds certain ideas to be true. Truth is vital for life, but Christian living is far more than the acceptance of Christian teaching. As Leander Keck points out, preaching is more than expounding a correct theology.

> We must see also the difference between *preaching a theology of grace and communicating a grace-full event with theological clarity*. Much more is at stake here than a word game. What matters is putting the news about Jesus in such a way that it reaches the hearer as a grace-event, as good news. The distinction, then, turns on the difference between communicating grace and advocating a concept called grace.
>
> Characteristically, Christian orthodoxy has preached grace. Yet hearing a theological point elucidated and

advocated is not yet hearing good news, gospel. Grace has not yet happened when it is explained. More often than not, such a sermon reaches the unconvinced hearer as a required idea. Actually, one should preach so that a new situation is created for the hearer, one in which he is grasped by grace.

A grace-event occurs when the word about Jesus reaches the hearer as good news for him.[14]

"The message of the gospel does not witness to a good idea to be believed, but to a good God who invites our surrender, trust and obedience."

THE LISTENER'S CONTINUED REACTION

"Just two things more: one regarding your message, and the other, concerning the 'message' your own manner sometimes conveys."

CHEAP GRACE?

"First the message. You put great stress on grace. You proclaim that God loves us more than we love ourselves, and that we can't do anything to get God to stop loving us. I'm all for proclamation of the grace of God; that's the yes I asked you for—but isn't this getting dangerously close to the cheap grace Bonhoeffer warned against in *The Cost of Discipleship?*"[15]

THE MESSAGE OF YOUR MANNER

"Second, I am sometimes troubled by the message communicated by your manner more than your words.

Who you are in attitude and manner confirms or contradicts the message being expressed by your words.

"Usually you seem to speak from where you live, but sometimes it seems like a mechanical performance. It's as if preaching is a part of your job and you are doing it because you have to. Then I wonder, How real to you is that of which you speak? I'm not accusing you of being a hypocrite, but do you sometimes preach without being personally involved in your message?"

THE PREACHER AGAIN RESPONDS TO THE LISTENER'S REACTION

ON CHEAP GRACE

"It is easier to respond to your first objection than to the second. I have no desire to proclaim cheap grace. It costs to love in this sinful world, and God, who loves the most, pays the highest price of all. The cross of Christ stands as a continual reminder of God's costly grace. E. Stanley Jones has stressed that whenever love meets sin a cross is raised up and that Jesus' 'outward cross that was lifted up in history is a sign of that inward cross that lies upon the heart of God.'[16]

"Grace can be regarded as cheap. We can live with the attitude expressed by the person who said, 'I love to sin and God loves to forgive, so we get along fine.' Such talk is blasphemy. It's like a husband saying, 'My wife will love me no matter what, so I do every unkind and unfaithful thing I can think of.' An attitude which takes love as an excuse for sin shows no gratitude for love and reveals contempt for the person who loves. But the fault in this case is not with the lover but with the person loved. Every time we love, we risk the possibility of our love being regarded cheaply, and God, who loves constantly, takes that risk every moment. We often take his gifts for granted and treat them as if they were our due. Such living witnesses to our cheapening of God's grace.

"Our failure to see the true worth of God's grace does not stop God from being gracious, nor should the possibility of our hearers taking the message of grace cheaply deter us from proclaiming it. We need to be vigilant in declaring God's holy love with awe and reverence so that we do not by word or manner cheapen it ourselves, but beyond that we leave the response to the hearer.

"We must especially resist the temptation to avoid cheap grace by substituting conditional grace. When we say, 'God will be gracious to you *if* you confess and repent and have faith,' and thereby imply that God is not gracious toward us as we are, we are proclaiming a conditional grace which in reality is not grace at all.

> The Gospel is not an offer of grace, salvation, forgiveness and sonship on certain conditions which "by God's help" we are to fulfill. . . . There is absolutely no condition of any kind, no demands or requirements as to the condition of the heart or soul in those to whom these free tidings come.[17]

"God does not love us only *if* we do this or don't do that, or only *if* we believe this or disbelieve that. God loves us as we are, with all our sins, doubts, and peculiarities.

"The solution to the cheap grace problem is in confrontation with ourselves as we are and with God as he reveals himself to be in Jesus Christ. When we see our helplessness to overcome our perversity and powerlessness, and come to trust God's life-giving mercy and power, the likelihood is not that we will regard his grace with contempt, but that we will instead be continually renewed in reverence and gratitude."

ON MANNER VERSUS MESSAGE

"Your confession of sometimes finding my manner of preaching to convey a message contrary to my words is very disturbing. There have been times after, or even during, a sermon when I've felt something was wrong and sensed the problem was more with me than with my message. Your comments give me the same distressed feeling as when I first read these words from Helmut Thielicke:

> If I am not mistaken, the man of our generation has a very sensitive instinct for routine phrases. Advertising and propaganda has thoroughly accustomed him to this. . . . Anybody who wants to know whether a particular soft drink is really as good as the advertising man on the television screen says it is cannot simply believe the phonetically amplified recommendations, but must find out whether this man actually drinks this soft drink at home when he is not in public. Does the preacher himself drink what he hands out in the pulpit? This is the question

that is being asked by the child of our time who has been burned by publicity and advertising.

The man of our time would certainly be doing an injustice to the pastor if he supposed that he might possibly be a hypocrite. I know a great number of ministers, but I do not know a single one who secretly swears by a "different brand of soft drink" from the one he is advocating. . . .

It is not sufficient for us that the preacher is subjectively imbued with the correctness of his conviction and that he is therefore not a conscious hypocrite. (We certainly do not think he is that disreputable.) In order to be able to form a judgment concerning his credibility (and here again we come back to the soft drink illustration) we would have to know whether he lives, whether he really "exists," in the house of the dogmas he proclaims.

This means that what the preacher says in the pulpit must have a relationship to what fills the rest of his existence. Sure, he is a nice, pleasant, affable fellow. But I ask you, when does anything about Christ come out in his ordinary human conversation? When is this name uttered quite naturally when he is talking to me about the weather or about my son? He is a man of culture. Whenever there is a problem play in movies or in the theater he is sure to be there. . . . When he talks about these things his voice has that natural and casual tone, which indicates that what is said has become a natural and obvious part of the intellectual organism. But when he talks about "sacred" things, the very timbre of his voice (though it has not a trace of "pulpit tone") shows that he is talking about something which has been brought in from some faraway region, something that now lies like a foreign body, like a meteor from another planet in the normal landscape of his life. . . .

The fact that he works hard on his preaching—that he studies the Bible, and ponders theological problems—this would still be no proof that he drinks his own "soft drink." All this could be, as we said, only a conditioned reflex, an effect of the categorical imperative which demands that he be faithful in his job. The question is rather whether he quenches his own thirst with the Bible, just as he satisfied the thirst of his intellectual and human interests in the theater or in association with his friends. If I see a breach, if I see no connection, between his Christian and his human existence—so argues the average person consciously or unconsciously—then I am inclined to accept the conclusion that he himself is not living in the house of his own preaching, but has settled down somewhere beside it, and that therefore the center of gravity in his life lies elsewhere.[18]

"I frankly shuddered at the thought of those words applying to me, and now your comment suggests they sometimes do. But what am I to do about it? This is not something to be corrected by learning a new homiletical technique. The problem is not in my preaching, it's in me. What I must need is nothing less than a continued and expanded conversion of my inner attitudes and values. I'd best listen to the message of my own sermons and preach to myself before, and as, I speak to you.

"I too need the gospel's yes and the law's no and I fear that I must especially need that no to break the shell of my pious professionalism. Your honest confrontation, added to Thielicke's statement, is that kind of no to me. It is a hard word which I am reluctant to accept. I see that I am desperately defensive of myself and my preaching, and that I'm afraid that my defenses will break down to expose my ignorance and pride. Yet I know that when we open our mouths we let others see into our hearts and minds and that there is no way any preacher can fool every listener for very long. I must often confess to being self-saving and self-serving in my preaching. I try to preach good sermons which will reward me with approval and appreciation, and in so doing am sometimes more of a performer than a proclaimer. I see that I should stop trying to preach good sermons and concentrate on sharing an honest message which seeks to do vital business in both my life and yours. I'm grateful to hear that you sometimes find that happening, and I pray that my attention may be called away from myself to the message Christ sends me to speak, and to you who come to listen, so that it may happen more and more."

CHAPTER THREE

How Should I Preach?

The Preacher asks, "How should I preach?"

The Listener replies: "As I understand your question, you are asking for specific suggestions concerning how to prepare and preach a sermon. You are wondering about where to start and how to proceed.

"As a listener who knows little about homiletical techniques, I will again attempt an answer from the perspective of how I want you to preach to me. I have the impression that many preachers are in trouble, not only for lack of technique, but for want of a clear understanding of the end product they wish to produce. Only after determining your destination can you select the roads to travel there. I will, therefore, list some of the characteristics of the most meaningful preaching I've heard and then let you preachers decide the best ways of preparing such sermons."

A LIVING EVENT

"As I do so, remember that when I describe a sermon I'm not talking about the words on paper. A sermon is the living event that happens when a preacher preaches. A written copy of the words spoken is not the living sermon, but only its verbal remains. We can, for example, profitably study the written 'corpses' of Luther's or Wesley's sermons, but only those who heard them preached experienced the living sermons."

CHARACTERISTICS OF VITAL SERMONS

"With this in mind, here are some of the characteristics of sermons which do vital business in my life:

(1) They are a means by which the Bible speaks to me. A significant sermon is an extension of a biblical text, reaching out to touch my life for the purpose of doing something in me and through me. The message of that text is more than something to be believed; it comes as a word to renew and reorder my life.

(2) Vital sermons speak to my condition and deal with issues related to my personal life. They do not leave me wondering, What has this to do with me? Some of the failure of sermons in this regard results from use of the abstract language such as talk about 'Man': 'Man is a sinner'—'God comes in search of Man,' etc. Who is that Man? Aren't we the sinners, and doesn't God come in search of us? But beyond use of impersonal language, other factors of approach and content make my experience with preaching either a vital personal encounter or an impersonal spectator sport.

(3) In terms of comprehensible and compelling communication, the most meaningful sermons come from preachers having direct, no-nonsense delivery. They look me in the eye and talk to me and with me. Some preachers speak more directly during the announcements than during the sermon. When urging us to help paint the church basement, they speak with the natural directness of intense personal conversation. But in the pulpit, they often read or recite a theological essay more suited for publication than proclamation. When this happens there is something wrong. Is it the result of the preacher's inner contradictions, discussed earlier, or is it also a sign of an incorrect approach and faulty process of preparation?

(4) Vital sermons are clear. The preacher deals with something in particular, and it is evident he has carefully ordered his thought. The sermon has direction and a clarity of expression which comes only from clarity of thought. When I can't understand a sermon, I wonder is it because the preacher is so profound or because he is so confused? Sometimes I'm quite sure the problem is not just my stupidity but the preacher's lack of clarity.

"Here, then, is my answer concerning how to preach: seek a process of preparation that results in sermons which are a clear, direct, personally relevant expression of the biblical witness."

THE PREACHER REFLECTS ON THE LISTENER'S REQUEST

The Listener has given a fourfold picture of a model sermon and left it to us to select the means of producing it. Being confronted with such a model reminds me of our young son's comment after our vacationing family had heard a sermon that captured us all. Looking up at me as we left the church, he asked, "Daddy, why don't you preach like that?" I could only reply, "I wish I could!"

We need models to guide us in our preaching, and the Listener's description leads us to seek means by which our sermons can be (1) more biblical, (2) more personal, (3) more directly communicated, and (4) more clearly ordered and expressed.

BE BIBLICAL

We are challenged to preach sermons which are "extensions of biblical texts reaching out to touch our lives." How can our sermons become more biblical in this sense?

We preachers need to approach the Bible from a preaching perspective, which recognizes that biblical preaching is not just talk about the Bible but is rather an expression of the message of the Bible to our lives. Helmut Thielicke speaks for all preachers when he says, "What happens in the pulpit must not turn out to be a lecture on Bible problems. . . . On the contrary, I must deliver the *message* of this text to people living today." [1]

WHAT DOES THIS TEXT WANT TO DO?

Therefore, we not only ask, What does this text say? but also, What does this text want to do? We think in terms of what James Randolph calls the "intentionality of the text."[2] The intentionality of the text reveals the specific possibility to which we preach. Our central purpose in preaching is not to explain the Bible, but to let our sermons be a means of grace to give life to our hearers. True textual preaching is not a lecture *on* a text but a sermon *from* a text which seeks to effect the possibility the text intends.

ON AND *FROM* ILLUSTRATED

As an illustration note two ways of dealing with the statement: "For by grace you have been saved through faith; and this is not your own doing, it is the gift of God—not because of works, lest any man should boast" (Eph. 2:8-9). One preacher might preach *on* the text and approach it primarily as a subject to be explained. His "sermon" will be a lecture explaining grace, faith, and works, and describing the relationship of each to the others. This sermon may be helpful. We need to have things explained and made clear. Such "preaching" can certainly be used by the creative Spirit of God as a means of grace to give new life to people. But note how another preacher might approach and preach *from* the text in a different manner. He thinks in terms of what the text intends and sees that the intention of the text is not only that people will understand that we are justified by grace through faith, but that *they will come to be* justified by grace through faith. He sees new life of faith in the grace of God as a real possibility for himself and each of his hearers. What he seeks to do in his sermon is not just *to explain* grace and faith, but *to so proclaim* the grace of God that faith will be born in the lives of his listeners. He will call them out of their self-saving efforts to attain their own salvation and call them into a life of abandonment to the gracious God who saves us without our help. Grace makes it possible for us to live a loved, forgiven, accepted life. When he preaches from this text, this preacher seeks to lead his hearers into the initial and continual fulfillment of this possibility in each of their lives.

SHED THE LIGHT OF THE BIBLE ON LIFE

This second preacher, who seeks to effect what his texts intend, is the more correct biblical expositor. With Fosdick, he sees that "the Bible is a searchlight not so much intended to be looked at as to be thrown upon some shadowed spot."[3] His chief aim in preaching is therefore not to shed light on the Bible but to shed the light of the Bible on life. In order to shed the light of the Bible on life, he will usually find it helpful and often essential to shed light on the Bible, but, for him, teaching about the text will not be an end in itself. He sees that being a Christian means new life to be lived and not just new information to be learned or old beliefs to be accepted. The information in his sermons will be offered as a means toward transformation of the lives of his hearers. Sometimes he will speak much about the text, sometimes hardly at all. His best sermon on repentance, for example, might not even use the word repentance but will so proclaim the grace of God and so expose our lack of trust and love that some who hear it will in fact repent.

SEEING POSSIBILITIES IN WHAT TEXTS INTEND

What was said earlier about preaching to the possibilities of people may seem to imply that we best begin sermon preparation by seeing an unfulfilled possibility in the lives of our hearers. This may sometimes be true. When there is a positive possibility crying to be met, we will often be wise to address ourselves directly to its fulfillment. If we know the Bible, texts will come to mind which shed light on this situation and give strength and direction to our hearers. There is nothing wrong with selecting a text and letting it work toward the fulfillment of a specific possibility, provided, of course, that this possibility is related to the true intention of the text. Even those committed to preaching "the text for the day" select texts for funeral sermons to fulfill possibilities of comfort and hope. In the same way the pastor who is sensitive to the lives of his people will sometimes select texts and prepare sermons to help lift them toward the actualizing of other specific possibilities.

However, we need help in discovering these specific possibilities, and the best revelation of our positive possibilities is found in the intention of biblical texts.

When we study passages of scripture in terms of what they want to do in us and through us, specific life possibilities open before us. Therefore, I believe the best place to begin in our preparation for preaching is with a biblical text.

Every exegetical tool at our command should be used to help us understand what the text says. But beyond that we ask of every text, What does this passage want to do? Seeing that goal, we then seek to preach gospel, law, and the great commission to fulfill in our hearers what this text intends.

BE PERSONAL

How can we meet our listener's request to keep our sermons relevant to his personal life? Certainly by using the personal language of direct discourse—we, us, you, and me—rather than the abstract Man of the theological classroom. But impersonal preaching is more than a language problem. It results from a wrong approach to our people and to the texts and themes of our preaching. We need life-situation preaching, which, as Ronald Sleeth points out, is not a type of preaching but an approach involved in all vital proclamation.[4]

TAKE HOLD ON THE "PREACHING END"

With a life-situation approach, we seek to take hold of every text and theme on what Halford Luccock called "its preaching end."[5] We deal with our sermon content in terms of the way it touches the lives of the people to whom we preach. We ask ourselves, How does this matter relate to me and to my people? Every vital text and issue has a near end where it touches life. Human suffering, for example, is not just an academic question to be discussed in the seminary classroom. Suffering is a life problem, and the person overwhelmed by suffering needs more than an abstract explanation of his misery. He needs a love and a power that can sustain him in hope and courage. We cannot explain everything, but we can proclaim the good news that the God of suffering love is with us in our pain as in our joy, and that he calls us to work with him to rid the world of every evil.

Anything that affects the lives of people is proper matter for Christian preaching. Issues related to war, prejudice, poverty, hunger, starvation, exploitation, waste of material and human resources, and the like belong in the pulpit. The wise preacher will sense that there are ways in which each of these matters is relevant for each of us. We are in some measure a part of these problems, and there are also ways by which we can become part of the cure. The Christian preacher seeks to speak the word of judgment against immoral policies of the church, state, and society, but he never forgets that our personal attitudes and actions are involved in both the perpetuation and the correction of those policies. His main emphasis is toward fulfillment of specific possibilities for Christian living. He will, therefore, seek to lead his people into new values and to encourage their personal action over against these evils.

Dealing with controversial issues in personal terms is more difficult and more dangerous than preaching abstractly. Few are angered by pious generalities with which they usually claim to agree. But when we get personal and talk about specific possibilities for change, some will be offended. When exposing wrong, we need to remember that we ourselves stand with our people under the judgment as well as the mercy of God. Most parishioners will be open to the correction of a preacher they believe to be sincerely sharing the judgment of God he feels upon his own as well as his hearers' failures, but they have little patience with the pompous pontificator who stands in the pulpit, "four feet above contradiction," as Paul Scherer used to say, and self-righteously tells off his congregation.

PERSONAL PREACHING—PASTORAL AND PROPHETIC

Preachers able to take prophetic stands on controversial issues without alienating half the congregation seem to be those who understand prophetic ministry to be an extension of pastoral ministry. Pastoral preaching expresses concern to give new life to those who are present. Prophetic preaching expresses this same pastoral concern for people present *or absent* who need our voice, vote, gifts, or action.

It is sometimes difficult to be both pastoral and prophetic at the same time, but when involved with controversial issues it is essential that the two be kept together. If in our concern for people far away we express contempt for those seated before us, we are unlikely to help anyone near or far. We best beware lest we take secret delight in scolding our people. Such delight is more a sign of contempt for our own congregation than of compassion for the oppressed of the earth. When our people sense we are standing with them under God's judgment and sharing what we believe the love of Christ compels us to say, they not only treat us more charitably but are also more open to be changed by our message. They realize that Christ sends us all to care for others beyond the circle of family, friends, and congregation. Prophetic preaching is really pastoral preaching on behalf of other people. As personal, pastoral-prophetic preachers we speak *to* those who hear us and *for* those who need us.

In prophetic as in pastoral preaching, we preach by the grace of God, remembering that love, peace, patience, kindness, goodness, and self-control are among the fruit of the Spirit. They are not the fruit of an angry preacher's scolding. We do not make the beans grow by pulling on them. As a farmer surrenders seed to the soil, we yield our sermons to our hearers, trusting God to give the growth.

As we seek a life-situation approach to all our preaching, we will preach to the problems, but above all to the positive possibilities of the life to which Christ invites and enables. We will attempt to relate the mercy and judgment of God so personally to ourselves and our hearers that we are repeatedly renewed in self-forgetful trust and self-giving love.

BE DIRECT

The third characteristic of our listener's model sermon relates to the preacher's manner of speaking. He appreciates sermons shared with the natural vitality and directness of intense personal conversation. Those words single out two qualities of central importance in all public speaking: naturalness and conversational quality.

NATURALNESS

It is helpful for us preachers to be reminded that public speaking is a natural extension of normal conversation. James Winans gives an imaginative illustration of this fact:

> Let us imagine all speeches and all memory of speech-making to be blotted out, so that there is no person in the world who remembers that he has ever made a speech, or heard one, or read one; and there is left no clue to this art. "Is this the end of speech-making?" Here comes a man who has seen a great race, or has been in a battle, or perhaps is excited about his new invention, or on fire with enthusiasm for a cause. He begins to talk with a friend on the street. Others join them, five, ten, twenty, a hundred. Interest grows. He lifts his voice that all may hear; but the crowd wishes to hear and see the speaker better. "Get up on this truck!" they cry; and he mounts the truck and goes on with his story or plea.

A private conversation has become a public speech; but under the circumstances imagined it is only thought of as a conversation, enlarged conversation. It does not seem abnormal, but quite the natural thing.

When does the converser become a speech-maker? When ten persons gather? Fifty? Or is it when he got up on the truck? There is, of course, no point at which we can say the change has taken place. There is no change in the nature or the spirit of the act; it is essentially the same throughout, a conversation adapted as the speaker proceeds, to the growing number of his hearers. There may be a change to be sure, if he becomes self-conscious; but assuming that interest in story or argument remains the dominant emotion, there is no essential change in his speaking. I wish you to see that speech-making, even in the most public place, is a normal act which calls for no strange, artificial methods, but only for an extension and development of that most familiar act, conversation.[6]

Would that this naturalness of public speaking were deeply burned into our understanding so as to help purge all traces of artificial pulpit oratory from our preaching.

One test of the naturalness of our preaching is to compare recordings of pulpit speech with that of other conversation. For example, is our manner of speech in the pulpit essentially the same as in the adult class?

In preaching workshops at Luther Theological Seminary, students often remain in the pulpit following their sermons to answer a few questions. Both sermon and post-sermon question/answer sessions are recorded on video-tape. A marked contrast between the student's sermon and post-sermon manner of speaking is often revealed. When this happens, the post-sermon manner is almost always more direct and meaningful.

Another test of naturalness is to be interrupted with a question during the sermon. When this happens we can sometimes actually feel ourselves shifting from a formal, if not artificial, preaching style into natural, direct communication.

Naturalness in pulpit communication is related to our view of preaching and of ourselves. Sometimes our concept of preaching is so high, and of self so low, that we do not dare be our ordinary selves when we attempt the lofty task of proclamation. Preaching is a high calling that prompts confession of inadequacy, but it does not call us to pretense and phony pulpit performance. God sends us to serve him with the gifts he has given. We need not pretend to be other than we are. We need only give God a chance to use us.

CONVERSATIONAL QUALITY

Lack of conversational quality is one of the central factors contributing to dreary pulpit communication. To speak with conversational quality does not mean to adopt a cozy, chatty style of speech. When we are speaking with conversational quality *we are thinking of our thoughts at the moment we say them.* James McCroskey describes this aspect of conversational speech as involving a speaker's "conscious awareness of the content of the words as they are uttered." It happens when the "speaker is thinking of his entire thought as he is presenting his message. He is presenting thoughts, rather than words."[7]

This understanding of conversational quality has great significance for the process of preparation, and we therefore underscore its importance. When speaking conversationally we are not thinking about ourselves or about our words. We are neither reading words off a page nor reciting sentences committed to memory. *In conversational speech our attention is upon our thought. We are thinking of our message as we share it.*

The absence of conversational quality is often illustrated by the memorized recitation delivered by a child at the Christmas program. The anxious child is usually more concerned with repeating the words than with sharing a message, and we preachers are sometimes much the same. As we preach, our thoughts are on the words rather than on the message. One difficulty with either reading sermons from a manuscript or reciting them from memory is that it is almost impossible to do either without being distracted from our thoughts to our words. We need a method of preparation that makes it as easy as possible for us to relive our thoughts at the moment we express them.

BE CLEAR

Someone has said that the three most important rules for the preacher are (1) Be Clear, (2) Be Clear, (3) Be Clear. This overstatement reflects our listener's concern that our sermons be clearly ordered and expressed.

THE IMPORTANCE OF CLARITY
FOR THE PREACHER

If clarity is important for those who listen, it is essential for us who preach. The reason many preachers feel dependent upon full manuscripts is not poor memory, but sermons so poorly ordered that it is impossible to remember them. Try recalling a list of random numbers: 7, 23, 4, 1, 248, 6, 219, 3, 86. We do not easily recall such lists, nor do we manage a similar list of randomly related sermon ideas. We must either read them or laboriously commit them to memory.

Now try a list of logically ordered numbers—5, 10, 15, 20, 25, 30, 35, 40. We can repeat these numbers an hour from now after just a glance. This is not to suggest sermons be artificially structured but to emphasize that a clearly ordered plan of development is essential.

The listener has asked for sermons which are a clear, direct, personal proclamation of the biblical message. With this model in mind, we turn to the specific process of preparing.

A PROCESS OF PREPARATION

Sermon preparation includes two tasks which overlap in time but differ in intention: (1) preparation *for* the sermon which involves gathering content from which the substance of the sermon will be drawn, (2) preparation *of* the sermon involving selection and ordering of thought into the specific plan of sermon development. Preparing a sermon is similar to preparing a dinner. The cook prepares *for* the dinner by shopping at a grocery store. Preparation *of* the dinner takes place in the kitchen, where the specific grocery items are selected, cooked, and combined. Without preparation *for* the meal there is no food to serve. Without preparation *of* the meal there is only a pile of groceries on the table.

Sermons, like dinners, need both preparations, and we preachers can fail at either or both. We may attempt to order our thoughts without having gathered enough food for a sermonic snack. Or we may set a bag of homiletical groceries before the congregation without having cooked the meal. Some of our preaching is so lacking in both preparation *for* and *of,* that our sermons are thin stew, served half cooked.

PREPARATION FOR THE SERMON

GENERAL PREPARATION FOR ALL SERMONS

In the widest sense, preparation *for* preaching includes our total learning and experience. When asked on rare occasion to speak on short notice, we might not decline for lack of time to prepare but might rather reply, "I've been preparing for this all my life."

Because preaching involves sharing a living message with living people we need continual general preparation that deepens understanding of both our people and our message. If Phillips Brooks and Harry Emerson Fosdick could not preach without in-depth contact with persons, we probably can not either. Preaching is enriched through visiting and counseling, and we do well to get involved with groups such as Alcoholics Anonymous and Emotions Anonymous, which help people face the problems and possibilities of life.

To have something to give, we need to be perpetual sponges soaking up insights from everything and everyone. Reading, deep and wide, including lifelong study of scripture, is essential. The portrait of a preacher with the Bible in one hand and the newspaper in the other should be the picture of us all.

SPECIFIC PREPARATION FOR THIS SERMON

Beyond such general preparation, we need to prepare *for* each sermon. This specific preparation usually begins with selection of a biblical text or a topic of concern upon which the biblical witness sheds light. I am grateful to be part of a tradition that encourages use of assigned texts for the church year. These texts are the church's gift to me, and I regard the listings not as a master slavishly to be obeyed but as a friend to help me in my work. As we live in scripture, we will with Fosdick see "text after text lift up its hands begging to be used."[8] At other times matters of concern will call for more topically centered sermons or a series developing a theme too big for a single sermon.

Robert McCracken, who succeeded Fosdick at Riverside Church in New York, kept a large loose-leaf preparation notebook. Half the book was used to record notations related to biblical texts from which he was planning to preach. The rest was dedicated to specific topics or concerns around which he was gathering material for future sermons.

Whether we preach from texts or on topics it is well to start early. It takes three weeks for a hen to hatch an egg, and it may take at least that long to hatch a sermon. During this brooding process, study the text itself before turning to commentaries. Knowledge of Greek and Hebrew is extremely helpful, but even if we must work with English translations we should discipline ourselves to study text and context on our own before turning to secondhand sources, which are useful to confirm, correct, and enrich our own findings.

THE "JOTTING" STAGE

The "preparation *for*" phase of sermon preparation might be called the Jotting Stage. As we study and ponder we jot down every thought, insight, bit of information, or suggested illustration that comes to mind which might relate to the sermon we shall eventually preach. During this stage we make no effort to order these ideas into a sermon plan. If a possible plan comes to mind it will be recorded as one item among the jottings. The purpose now is to stock the shelves; later we shall prepare the meal. It is better to gather supply sufficient for several meals, and of necessity leave most of it on the shelves, than to invite people to dinner without enough to feed the guests.

All through this process we remember we are preparing *to preach from* the text and not *to lecture* about the text. We shall therefore seek the intention, as well as the content, of the passage and shall look for ways of letting the text fulfill its purpose in our lives. Whether centered on text or topic we will to "take hold on the preaching end" where it touches our lives, and shall see it in the context of the yes, no, and go of gospel, law, and great commission.

PREPARATION OF THE SERMON

Having accumulated several pages of disconnected jottings we find our attention shifting from preparation *for* the sermon to preparation *of* the sermon. Various themes and possible plans of development will have suggested themselves, and we now begin selecting and ordering our thought into the specific plan for this sermon. We ask ourselves, Out of all these jottings what is the most important message I have been given to share? Having selected that message, or having let it select us, we go on to ask, How can I best order the ideas essential to this message so that they can be clearly shared and clearly received?

THE "THINK" STAGE

We could call the phase of selection and ordering of thought the Think Stage of preparation. Thinking is obviously important at all stages of preparing but is especially significant at this point. We are tempted to move too quickly from the Jotting Stage to the preaching or writing of the sermon. Two kinds of preachers come close to skipping the Think Stage altogether. One type ad-libs in the pulpit. Having made some jottings this preacher enters the pulpit with no clearly developed plan of thought and speaks out of his head until the time is up or he can think of nothing more to say. The other type ad-libs in the study. These preachers might never dare go into the pulpit without a full manuscript, but they prepare that manuscript by ad-libbing at the typewriter. Their thoughts move their fingers in a kind of free association, stream-of-consciousness development until a sufficient number of pages has been filled with words, whereupon they declare the sermon to be completed. Many sermons composed in this way are so lacking in clarity and progression of thought that there is nothing holding them together but the paper on which they are written.

SPECIFIC SUGGESTIONS

The Listener desires direct, personal, clearly ordered communication. He wants the preacher to look him in the eye and yet know what he is saying. We have stressed that one goal of preparing is to enable the preacher to think his thoughts while sharing them. The following are specific suggestions for preparation *of* the sermon which can help toward such preaching.

First, four suggestions concerning selection of the theme.

(1) Determine that this sermon will be thematic as well as textual. Plan to have one central message or "big truth."[9] Helmut Thielicke states:

> I choose this . . . textual-thematic kind of preaching and for three different reasons.
>
> First, in this way one remains within the text and allows it to be an end in itself. . . .
>
> Second, this . . . helps the preacher to achieve order and clarity. . . .
>
> Third, this method is also more helpful to the hearer. He retains it better and can more readily pass it on to others. . . . The thematic sermon is helpful most of all to hearers who are interested in a question and perhaps have no desire to listen to any biblical exposition whatsoever.[10]

(2) Work to narrow this theme to manageable dimensions. Plan to deal with something concretely rather than with everything abstractly.

(3) Preach on themes that "grab" you. Preach to yourself as you preach to others but remember that some people are different from you. Seek also to speak to them.

(4) See your theme in relation to your purpose. Why preach this sermon? What specific possibility of new life might this message help fulfill?

Next, twelve suggestions concerning the ordering process.

(1) Think in terms of Introduction, Development, and Conclusion. Write these words on a sheet of paper.

```
┌─────────────────────────────────┐
│ Introduction                    │
│                                 │
│                                 │
│ Development                     │
│                                 │
│                                 │
│                                 │
│                                 │
│                                 │
│ Conclusion                      │
│                                 │
│                                 │
│                                 │
└─────────────────────────────────┘
```

Whatever the content, we have to begin with something, develop something, and end with something.

(2) On this page, sketch out a rough-draft, preliminary plan of one way you might present the sermon.

    a. Follow Paul Scherer's suggestion to use pencil and eraser all through this ordering process.[11] This helps free us from becoming locked into the form of preliminary drafts. Penciled statements seem less sacred and are easily altered. Some preachers do the preliminary ordering at the chalkboard for the same reason.

b. Remember that you are *selecting* and *ordering ideas*. Make no attempt at this stage to write out exactly how you will eventually express these ideas. Think in terms of chunks of thought and work to see the big picture of total development. If each of your major ideas were a physical chunk of thought your plan of development might look something like this:

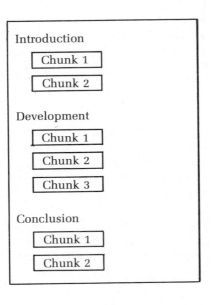

(3) Let yourself *see* the relationship between your major and minor ideas.

a. One way to do this is to use a form of reversed indenting. Let the main points really stand out.

Introduction
    1st Main Point of Introduction
      sub-points
    2nd Main Point of Introduction
      sub-points

Development
    1st Main Point of Development
      sub-point
      sub-point
        sub-sub point
        sub-sub point
    2nd Main Point of Development
      sub-point
        sub-sub point
      sub-point
        sub-sub point

Conclusion
    1st Main Point of Conclusion
    2nd Main Point of Conclusion

b. Another way to help *see* the development is to use numbers and letters. With clear indenting the numbers and letters are not necessary, but they may be helpful. It has been said that an intelligent person is one who knows the difference between big *A* and little *a*. He sees the difference between a major and a minor idea. Some such form as the following may help us to *see* that difference.

```
Introduction
    I.
    II.

Development
    I.
        A.
            1.
                a.
                b.
            2.
        B.
    II.   Etc.

Conclusion
    I.
    II.
```

(4) Review and rework.

After having scratched out this first, one-page, preliminary plan step back from it and ask how you could do it differently. Do your main points express main aspects of the big truth you want to share? Are these points in the best order? Could you reverse them? Leave some out? What if one of the main points became the main theme or if you were to begin with what you are considering for the conclusion?

(5) Develop alternative plans.

Continued reflection will often suggest several alternative plans of development. Rough out several one-page preliminary plans. If these are done by midweek you can sleep on them.

(6) Select a plan.

When you continue preparation begin by reviewing your jottings. Ask if you are clear on theme and purpose. Then go back to review the preliminary plans. Usually one, or a combination of a couple, will "grab" you as the way to go. Or you may think of a whole new approach and order of development which you quickly sketch out as your first-choice plan.

(7) Now flesh it out.

Having selected the plan, flesh it out into a several-page preliminary *detailed* outline. You are still ordering ideas and arranging thoughts, so do not worry about how you will say it. Be sure that you will have some specific things worth saying.

Stay with the threefold division of introduction, development, and conclusion. Use some pattern such as reverse indenting, possibly combined with numbering and lettering, to let yourself *see* the development all the way. When completed, such a preaching outline might be four, five, or more pages long with perhaps a half page devoted to introduction, one-fourth page to conclusion and the rest to the development.

While fleshing out this plan, draw a line down the right side of the page a couple of inches in from the edge to provide a margin in which to jot ideas that come to mind but which do not fit in the section being developed. When completed, the first page of this draft will look something like page 84. The outline is on the left with the additional jottings in the right margin.

(8) Prepare the final detailed plan for proclamation.

To ensure complete ordering of thought, and to facilitate clarity in expression of that thought, I find it helpful to prepare a final detailed outline in which parts of the sermon are virtually written out in full. I am especially concerned that the introduction, conclusion, and sections of central content be expressed clearly. The aim of such writing is not to prepare a manuscript that will be read but to be certain these thoughts can be communicated clearly.

Remember again that you are not preparing a statement for publication, you are preparing *yourself* to relive your thoughts at the mo-

Introduction

   I. _____   _____

                       _____   _____

                       _____   _____

  II. _____   _____

                       _____   _____

                       _____   _____

                       _____   _____

Development

   I. _____   _____

                       _____   _____

                       _____   _____

                       _____   _____

                       _____   _____

                       _____   _____

                       _____   _____

                       _____   _____

                       _____   _____

  II. _____   _____

                       _____   _____

ment of utterance. Thoughts and words are bound up together. If you have wrestled to find words to clearly express a central thought, those words should not be lost. Write them into the detailed outline in full sentence form. Other sections such as personal illustrations and examples need not be written out in full, although to keep concise, wordy preachers are well advised to do so.

After you have worked out this detailed plan from start to finish, it will be possible to *see* the sermon development down to the sub-points. You are able to step back, so to speak, and see the woods *and* the trees. The overall pattern of progressive thought and detailed development of each section will be visible. The total plan will be a rough, but clear, penciled structure with erasures and reworded portions. Some parts will be written out. The rest will be shorter statements that indicate insights, illustrations, and experiences. There will be no gaps left to be filled by impromptu ad-libbing. The whole and the parts are the result of a careful and often agonizing struggle to order the ideas in a clear, progressive way. Changes may be made up to time of delivery, but when the detailed outline is prepared, the essential work of selecting and ordering has been completed.

The preparation of this detailed plan is the

preparation of the sermon content. There is no need to prepare a formal, typewritten manuscript. If the public or publisher wants a manuscript, prepare it after preaching.

(9) Prepare preaching notes.

You may use the detailed outline in the pulpit. Because it lets you see the chunks of thought you will not read it, but will use it to help you to recall and relive those thoughts as you share them. It is often better, however, to prepare an as-brief-as possible but as-long-as-necessary set of preaching notes to help you in the pulpit. Include key words or phrases that trigger thoughts in your mind. Write in some of those precious statements you want "just so," but do not fall so in love with every word that you have to read them all. Risk having some awkward sentences, but do not risk failing to speak to your people.

(10) Get on top of your stuff.

Having decided what you will take with you to the pulpit, use your time to get on top of your stuff. You may go over it out loud or subvocalize it in your head. Either way, you will be attempting not to memorize the words but to master the thought in detail so that its communication can be conversational and direct. Without memorization, you will establish grooves of expression in your mind so that when you preach at two services, the sermons will be almost the same in wording as in thought. If you forget something it will usually be a minor point. Such forgetfulness is insignificant compared to the tragedy of preachers who read sermons for years without really communicating with their people.

(11) Plan for eyeball-to-eyeball encounter.

If you are so accustomed to speaking with a full manuscript that you fear attempting another method, try two things: (1) Write the manuscript in full-sentence outline form that lets you see the chunks of thought, and use your outline-manuscript as a full set of notes to remind you of your thoughts more than your words. (2) Be brave enough to try sharing your illustrations, examples, and personal experiences from your head rather than off the page.

Helmut Thielicke urges this kind of preaching:

Just as in our prayers we do not need to use the carefully polished fair copy but are allowed to follow the "rough draft"—so in preaching we certainly do not need to weigh our words with the precision scales by which the legalists and formalists allow themselves to be tyrannized, but may rather assume that hazards and risks of speech to which we expose ourselves in natural, everyday conversation. . . . The man who will not utter anything that is not guarded and "safe" is not reckoning with him who is able from "stones to raise up children to Abraham" This passion to safeguard ourselves is not inspired by the Holy Spirit; it is based merely upon fleshly anxiety.

The witness must venture something and dare not be afraid of the chips that fly as he hews. The discipline and the hard application must be taken care of *before* the witness begins to speak. But once he begins to speak, he must be free to venture and expose himself without defense. There is no real witness that is not utterly defenseless.[12]

Imagine a ship builder so concerned to build sturdy ships that he constructs them of such heavy steel plate that they sink when launched. Like that ship builder, we sometimes launch sermons so heavily weighted with concern for every word that they sink between pulpit and front pew.

Proper precaution against forgetfulness is one thing, fretful anxiety is another. There is something wrong with a man who is so fearful of his pants falling down that he wears two belts and three pairs of suspenders. There is something wrong with us if we are afraid to get into the pulpit without every word typed out before us. To all who have such fears, I plead with you to risk it. Be like the brave youngster who abandons his tricycle for a two-wheeler and stays with it in spite of falls until he gets the knack of it. You will find new joy in preaching, and your hearers will thank you for it.

(12) Try a preaching notes notebook.

My own practice is to use a 9½-by-6-inch loose-leaf, 3-ring notebook in which I place my penciled preaching outlines. By starting on the back of the first page I have two pages of notes before me without having to turn a page. (See illustration in Appendix I, page 116.) When properly prepared, these two pages should be all the notes we need. But the main thing is not the number of pages but the way we use them. When we are comfortably on top of our material, taking four to six pages of detailed preaching notes into the pulpit need not be distracting to us or to our hearers. We should discipline ourselves to look at our notes only as often as necessary to get our bearings, and should not take refuge in them as an escape from looking at our people.

ANY SHORTCUTS?

Is all this necessary? Many with a gift of gab in the pulpit or a gift for fluency at the typewriter can turn out sermons with less expenditure of time and thought. But is there really any substitute for some such process of careful selection, ordering, and re-ordering of ideas? I believe this process is the most direct route to the goal of an ordered body of thought which we can relive as we share it. As you begin to think in terms of ordering ideas and arranging chunks of thought you will often be surprised at how quickly you can sketch out a half dozen alternative preliminary plans. At other times you will struggle for hours to come clear in your own mind as to exactly what you are trying to share and how best to order it. Such frustration is the fault not of the process but of the complexity of life and our limited ability to think clearly. We must guard against any method of preparation which lets us settle for sermons which are a sloppy collection of loosely related thoughts.

A PREPARATION PROCESS CHECKLIST

Many other suggestions could be included concerning details of the preparation process. To share some of these, here is a personal checklist which I try to keep in mind.

Checklist questions regarding the sermon introduction:

(1) Do my opening thoughts relate to the personal lives of my hearers? Is there anything in the introduction to prompt someone to say, "I want to hear this because it sounds important to me."

(2) Does this introduction lead into the central theme or big truth? Does it, like the front sign on a bus, tell the direction we are going?

(3) Does this introduction indicate the connection between the biblical text and the big truth? Am I starting with talk about the Bible unrelated to the lives of my hearers? Would it be better to begin with the area of life to which the text speaks?

(4) Does this introduction enable me personally to get off to a comfortable start? Do these opening thoughts set the tone for the entire sermon by

lending themselves to expression in a natural, conversational manner?

Checklist questions regarding the sermon development:

(1) Does one central big truth control the development of this sermon?

(2) Does each main point clearly express an aspect or implication of this big truth? Have I had the courage to leave out pet thoughts which have little connection with the central theme?

(3) Does the plan of development rise naturally from the content, or am I trying to squeeze it into an unnatural form? Am I letting content shape structure, or am I attempting to impose a pattern on my material?

(4) Does everything I am planning to say relate to the lives of my hearers? Will this be worth one's time to hear? Does this message have potential for opening possibilities of new life in grace?

(5) Do I have clear "handles" on the main points to make it easy for me and my hearers to recognize and recall them? Have I stated these main points in the language of the main theme so that there will be no unnecessary confusion?

(6) Are my connections clear? Have I included adequate "turn signals" so that my listeners will not be lost or left behind when I turn a corner?

(7) Is the substructure clearly ordered, or do I have several clear main points with rambling in between?

(8) Am I planning to express everything in personal
     terms and to be specific and concrete rather than
     general and abstract? Do I have clear illustra-
     tions and examples?
(9) Am I relating to the social and corporate, as well
     as the individual, implications of the message?
(10) Am I keeping everything in the context of the
     central message of God's grace toward us in
     Jesus Christ our Lord?

Some checklist questions regarding the sermon
conclusion:

(1) Does the planned conclusion call the hearers
     out of themselves and into new possibilities of
     life in grace? Does it underscore the pardon and
     power that make new life possible?
(2) Is a summary necessary, or would it be redun-
     dant?
(3) Am I ending with a question or prescription that
     will only lead my hearers into futile self-
     preoccupation and self-striving?
(4) Does this conclusion lead into prayer? (Paul
     Scherer maintained that a sermon should
     prompt the hearers to pray and that the preacher
     should follow the sermon with prayer.)

One checklist question concerning the whole sermon: Does what I am planning to do in this sermon
stand the light of Phillips Brooks' admonition "Care
not for your sermon, but for your truth and for your
people"?[13] Am I preparing to preach a great or good

sermon so people will think well of me, or am I preparing to share a vital message which can be a means of grace giving new life?

To illustrate this process of preparation, an example of the stages involved in the preparation of a specific sermon is included in Appendix I, beginning page 102.

IN THE PULPIT

As Brooks suggests, the best pulpit communication results from our forgetting ourselves and remembering just two things: our truth and our people. Self-preoccupation is a curse of preaching. As the purpose of preaching is to call people out of self-centeredness into self-surrender and self-giving, so also the call of the Lord invites us to let go of ourselves and to preach with the abandon of self-forgetfulness.

The best delivery is that which calls no attention to itself. We should not be unduly proud when people praise our delivery. That may be a compliment from people who feel we speak meaningfully, or a criticism that we are only smooth performers. The best compliment is not "I heard a great sermon" but "I met a great God." As George Buttrick said, "There are no great preachers; there is only a great gospel that bids us to proclaim it."[14] Those words might well be taped into our pulpits for us to see when we stand to preach.

RESPOND TO YOUR OWN CONTENT

Correct emphasis in preaching is not contrived or forced; it is the preacher's alive, natural response to the message he is sharing. Many student preachers are too inhibited in this regard, and sometimes speak of matters of life and death as if they were of no importance. Much of this apparent lack of enthusiasm comes from fear which restricts natural expressiveness. We may feel we are giving much emphasis when in fact we are so up-tight little of that felt zest shows on the outside. Viewing oneself on video tape is often a revelation in this regard. Students viewing their classroom sermons often comment in effect, "I really felt excited preaching this sermon but seeing this tape makes it seem like a cure for insomnia."

GIVE YOUR BEST SELF A CHANCE

Other students get defensive and say, "That's the way I am!" But, thanks be to God, we do not need to stay as we are! We can be changed! We do not need to settle for dullness. Paul Scherer told his students that James Stewart, whom he described as "the best preacher now preaching in the English language," was a reserved person who "opened like a flower in the sun" when he began to preach.[15] This is not hypocrisy but an alive, natural response to the message of Christ. It is phony to fake feelings we do not have, but it is also a form of hypocrisy to suppress expression of the urgency we feel.

If possible, we should see ourselves preach via video tape or at least listen carefully to some of our recorded sermons. It is often especially helpful to review sermons preached some months previously. We hear these more objectively than the one just preached. If the verdict from such self-encounter is, "There is more life in me than in my sermons," it is often helpful to break deliberately the habit of reserve. If, for example, the video tape reveals a preacher with hands glued to the pulpit, we should deliberately plan to let go of it the next time we preach. Doing this may not feel natural at first, but it can be a first step toward a freedom of expression that is much more natural than being physically stuck to the pulpit.

LET GO OF YOURSELF

The same principle applies vocally. We may deliberately have to break the old pattern of speech before we can begin to be naturally free and responsive. We can pick some places in our next sermon (sections relating personal experiences, examples, and illustrations may be the easiest place to start) where we can plan to really let go in free, direct, personal sharing. As we preach with a bit of abandon in these sections we will grow in freedom to share the whole sermon with natural enthusiasm. We need to "let go" of ourselves as well as of our pulpits, and to let the meaning of our messages grab us. Life in the grace of God is a lively business, and we need to let ourselves respond to what we are saying.

DO NOT IMPOSE EMPHASIS

A video tape encounter or an honest friend may reveal that the problem is not lack of zest but a pattern of enthusiasm which we impose on our material. Some actually seem to follow the suggestion: If your point is weak, shout loudly. The exact oppposite is true. If your point is strong, emphasize it strongly. In every sermon some things are more important than others. If we are in living touch with our message as we are sharing it, and are not inhibited by the fears noted above, correct emphasis should come naturally without being planned or contrived. Proper enthusiasm arises from the content. Phony emphasis is imposed upon the content. Some preachers shout or whisper, smile or frown, no matter what they are saying. If we have developed an artificial pulpit pattern we need to be confronted and corrected.

TRY SOMETHING DIFFERENT

On occasion we can get out of the pulpit and give the sermon from the chancel or center aisle. Some pulpits are so removed in height or distance from the congregation that it would be well if they were seldom used at all. Aisle preaching can be a gimicky performance, but it can also be a means of bridging the gap between pulpit and pew.

To further preaching partnership we can also try some give-and-take dialogue sermons. The pastor and a lay person can have a chancel dialogue, or several lay people may enter the dialogue from the chancel or the pews. A dialogue sermon needs as careful preparation as any other and may fall as flat. Like other sermons they are best well planned, but not canned.[16]

In most congregations the mainstay of preaching will, and should, continue to be the preacher's proclamation of the gospel. Do not abandon proclamation in favor of open forums and group discussions. Experiment imaginatively to bring new meaning to your congregation's preaching, but never forget that our call to Christ is to proclaim the gospel. Let group interaction be a supplement to, and not a substitute for, gospel proclamation.

THE LISTENER RETURNS TO ASK FOR PARTNERSHIP IN PREACHING

"Like golfers driving golf balls in the dark, you preachers need help to know how you are doing. You need affirmation and appreciation as well as confrontation and correction. We listeners also need more involvement in the preaching process and therefore urge you to invite our sermon feed-back and feed-in.

"We could keep the pew racks supplied with sermon reaction cards." (See p. 98.)

"We could occasionally use a half page bulletin insert." (See p. 99.)

"Feed-back groups of persons invited to share reactions directly with the preacher or indirectly via a tape recording of the sermon discussion session could also be helpful for both preacher and hearers. Feed-in sessions involving laypersons in study and discussion of upcoming texts and themes could contribute a significant dimension to the preaching process. For

Sermon Reactions?
Preaching Suggestions?

To help make preaching a two-way street please write
your sermon reactions (positive and negative) and
suggestions on this card and return it with the offering or
hand to an usher. You need not sign your name. Thank
you.

Please use reverse side if needed

Partnership in Preaching

You are invited to be a partner in the preaching process. Please share your sermon reactions and suggestions on this form. Return on offering plate, hand to usher, or mail to church. You need not sign your name.

What did you appreciate in this sermon?

What detracted?

Suggestions for better preaching?

Please use reverse side for more reactions and suggestions and to list questions, concerns, texts, or topics you would like considered in future sermons. Thank you for your help.

this partnership to be successful you preachers must be open in encouraging us hearers to tell it like it is, and we reactors will need to be honest and specific in sharing our views."

THE PREACHER REFLECTS ON THE LISTENER'S REQUEST FOR FEED-BACK AND FEED-IN

Partnership in preaching can be extremely helpful to the preacher, especially if the listener's comments are kind, honest, and specific. We preachers need all the help we can get, and only the hearers can tell if we are "hitting the green." One of the best ways for us to hear ourselves is to listen to our listeners. As preachers and hearers we can help each other by encouraging feed-back and feed-in.

While affirming the practice of partnership in preaching, a few reservations seem in order. Some feed-back comments may do more harm than good. General negative reactions are especially destructive. General positive reactions give encouragement to continue, but to be told that "your sermons are dull" or "simple-minded" without any specific indication of cause or cure only tempts the preacher to give up. Specific corrections and suggestions are much easier to accept and adopt.

We also remember that our hearers are not the final judge of our preaching. We are called of God to proclaim his message in Christ, and we need beware lest we sell our sermonic souls for the pottage of people's praise. When the views of our people tempt us to compromise correct convictions we pray for courage to say with Peter and the Apostles, "We must obey God rather than men" (Acts 5:29). Feed-back and feed-in do not reduce our personal responsibility for preaching, but they can help us fulfill it.

Laypersons and pastors are therefore encouraged to invite each other to initiate and maintain specific procedures for sharing feed-back and feed-in. With openness from the preacher and kind honesty from the listeners, preaching can become a partnership of mutual helpfulness.[17]

APPENDIX I

An Illustration
of the Preparation Process

The following is an example of the stages involved in preparing a specific sermon.

PREPARATION FOR THE SERMON

This sermon began with the decision to preach from Colossians 1:24-29.

> Now I rejoice in my sufferings for your sake, and in my flesh I complete what is lacking in Christ's afflictions for the sake of his body, that is, the church, of which I became a minister according to the divine office which was given to me for you, to make the word of God fully known, the mystery hidden for ages and generations but now made manifest to his saints. To them God chose to make known how great among the Gentiles are the riches of the glory of this mystery, which is Christ in you, the hope of glory. Him we proclaim, warning every man and teaching every man in all wisdom, that we may present every man mature in Christ. For this I toil, striving with all the energy which he mightily inspires within me.

THE JOTTING STAGE

Preparation for this sermon started with exegetical study including time for brooding over the text as a mother hen broods over her nest of fertile eggs. During this period of study and brooding, several pages of disconnected notes were jotted down. At this stage, no attempt was made to order them into a sermon.

Among many more jottings, those for our sample sermon included notations such as:

on v. 25, Paul considered his ministry a gift—note his purpose: "To make word fully known." What if Paul didn't write Colossians??? Checked commentaries on authorship—concluded it's essentially Pauline, no problem for preaching—can relate passage to Paul's self-understanding of ministry

on v. 27, "God chose"—initiation with God-Grace

on v. 28, Again note purpose: "present every man mature in Christ." Here's the intention of the text. In what does this maturity consist? Can I preach to help make such maturity possible?

on v. 29, "I toil, striving—but not own strength—"with all energy he inspires within." Note from Greek text, It's really God or Christ working "in me in power." Luther's comment that the whole way of life for the Christian person consists of two things—trust in God and love neighbor—relates here: Christian life is both passive—yielded in trust to God, and active—busy in service to people.

SELECTION STAGE

While brooding over these jottings a sermon idea began to hatch. Items such as those noted above began to stand out on the jotting pages, and I started thinking of Paul's ministry and of our own lives in light of verse 29. Mature Christian life is "toil" and "striving," but it is not all self-effort. God is powerfully at work within. I decided to try and preach on a theme related to "Our working and God's working," with the purpose of preaching to the possibility that our lives, like Paul's, can involve a wedding of our efforts and God's energy.

PREPARATION OF THE SERMON

This led into the beginning stages of the preparation of the sermon itself. The first rough-draft preliminary plan prepared on Tuesday looked something like the following outline. Using a pencil all the way from the first preliminary plan to the final preaching notes allowed for easy alteration.

FIRST PRELIMINARY PLAN

Introduction
   1. Relate to hearer's experience of Christian life as struggle—work—striving and at same time—trust—rest in God
   2. Connect to text—especially v. 29—picture two sides of Paul's life—much toil—but by God's energy

3. How about us? Life all own striving? All rest in God? How go together?

Development

1. The danger of life being all self-centered struggle
   a) work righteousness
   b) idolatry of self
   c) ultimate futility of self-trust
2. The danger of life being all rest in God
   a) using God—"cheap grace"
   b) uselessness to others
   c) danger to selves—miss life we were born to live
3. The combination of our work and God's energy
   a) what God does
      gives life—strength
      sustained by Holy Spirit—love—fruit of the Spirit
   b) what we are to do
      (1) work as we rest—trust God, serve others not just selves
      (2) Luther sums it up: Trust God—Love neighbor

Conclusion

1. Examples: Ship and swimmer—rest and work at same time
2. Promise of grace—God's power as well as mercy makes life of rest and work possible for us.

In retrospect this outline looked "lecturish" with the gospel message tagged on at the end.

Sometime in the midst of wrestling with the relation-

ship between our work and God's work I recalled
hearing E. Stanley Jones tell of his reply to a person
who asked him to give the secret of his lifelong vitality.
Jones gave the credit to "grace, grass, and gumption."
The grass referred to some kind of vitamin pills made
from grain sprouts. Since I was not interested in
peddling vitamins and since grass now refers to
marihuana, that part of Jones' reply was set aside. Grace
and gumption, however, seemed to sum up the two
sides of the Christian life I was trying to deal with in
the sermon. This led to a second rough-draft outline
worked up on Wednesday or Thursday.

SECOND PRELIMINARY PLAN

Introduction
  1. Stanley Jones—credited life primarily to "grace
     and gumption"
  2. Paul—in effect does the same—v. 29
     a) "I toil, striving"—gumption
     b) God's energy within—grace
  3. How about us? Do we live by grace? By gump-
     tion? Or both?
Development
  1. Christian life is life by grace
     (While pondering the meaning of living by grace,
     I recalled Reinhold Niebuhr's discussion of the
     "Biblical Doctrine, Grace" in *The Nature and
     Destiny of Man* and made a jotting in the margin
     to check his comments.)
     a) Grace is "the mercy of God toward us"

    b) Grace is also "the power of God in us"[1]
       (1) Paul's experience II Cor. 12:9
          Grace sufficient when weak then strong
       (2) promise of grace—invites trust, grace—makes faith possible
          We can set our "troubled hearts at rest [and] trust in God always." (John 14:1 NEB)
    c) transition—Christian life—always trust, but not just trust—Luther quote on trust and love

2. Christian life is life with gumption
    a) saved not to loaf but to serve
       (1) Grace sets us free *from* self-serving *for* service
       (2) Since we need not save ourselves we can help save others
    b) in Christ God says—come to me, find rest; also says—go for me, get to work
    c) the needs of others call us to toil by God's energy—grace and gumption are to go together

3. Challenges calling for lives of gumption sustained by grace (get specific, give examples etc.)
    a) in personal relations with people—family etc.
    b) in work with church and community
    c) in world—work for justice, not just charity

Conclusion
1. Sum up with illustration of ship or swimmer—maybe make it a lifeguard who does two things at same time
    a) rests in the water

   b) works with all might to reach and rescue
      persons in trouble
2. So too Christ calls us to rest in grace and to work
   with gumption.
   a) grace—invites rest and gives strength
   b) needs of people—call for gumption in service
This seemed less of a lecture, although it still tended
in that direction, and it did avoid a tag-end gospel
proclamation; but it looked quite general, and I
wondered how to relate grace and gumption more
specifically to our life situations. Another plan
suggested itself and became the third rough-draft
outline, worked out on Thursday or Friday.

THIRD PRELIMINARY PLAN

Introduction
   1. Jones—grace and gumption, together
   2. Paul—Col. 1:29—again grace and gumption
   3. How about us? To check us out let's look at four
      exhibits A-B-C-D
      Ask as viewing each—Is this a picture of my life?
Development
   1. Exhibit A: The person who lives *with neither
      grace nor gumption*
      a) neither dependent nor dependable, neither
         responsive nor responsible
      b) has given up on God and on self
      c) Do we fit? not all the time; sometimes?
   2. Exhibit B: The person who lives *with gumption
      without grace*

a) going concern—hard-working—successful—honored
b) something wrong inside, strain—tense; much gumption—little grace
c) Does it fit us?
   (1) often fits us preachers—may have feverish activity for God with little trust in God
   (2) may fit others—under compulsion to succeed; may succeed in living life of gumption without grace
3. Exhibit C: The person who lives *by grace without gumption*
   a) many A and B types outside the church; most C types likely in the church
   b) these people rest upon the grace of God but in rest have gone to sleep—knowing they need not work to save selves, have forgotten to work to save others
   c) Do we see ourselves here?
      (1) Do we thank God for his blessings while neglecting our responsibilities?
      (2) Do we listen to "come to me?" but turn aside from "go for me?"
      (3) Do we rejoice in Eph. 2:8-9 but forget v. 10?
      (4) Do we live by John 3:16 but neglect I John 3:16?
   d) If so, we may be living by grace without gumption.
      (1) need wake up to fact—grace is not given to sustain us in greedy self-content

       (2) grace—not just God holding our hand, but strengthening our arms for service

    4. Exhibit D: The person who lives *by grace with gumption*

      a) This brings us back to people like E.S. Jones and Apostle Paul

      b) They live out the kind of mature life we see in Jesus
        (1) "the man for others"—gumption
        (2) also "the man of God"—grace

      c) Luther sums it up
        (1) trust in God—grace
        (2) love neighbor—gumption

      d) Grace makes *passive trust* possible
        (1) invite abandonment—rest in God—John 14:1 NEB
        (2) Christian life—constant trust in God's mercy and power

      e) Grace makes *active love* possible—gumption is born of grace
        (1) freed from having to save selves—are free to serve others
        (2) Christian life is like
          (a) ocean liner—at rest and at work to serve
          (b) lifeguard—rests, yet toils to save

Conclusion

    1. Where do we fit? Likely no one exhibit all the time

      a) Am sure all wish to be more like D

      b) Whatever we are like now, we can live lives of more grace and more gumption

    (1) God loves us more than we love ourselves.
His power is with us to lift and use. Life in
grace is possible.

    (2) Some people need us—these are for us the
most important people in the world. Their
needs call for our gumption.

2. Loved by God—needed by people—we say with
Paul, "For this I toil, striving with all the energy
which he mightily inspires within me."

3. Thanks be to God—in our lives, too, grace and
gumption can go together.

Post-Sermon Prayer—for trust to live by grace and for
love to work with gumption.

With Sunday drawing near, I decided to go with this
plan. After working over the third rough draft, I
prepared the final *detailed* preparation outline. Much
of the sermon was virtually written out in penciled
outline form. But it was not a manuscript and was to be
neither memorized nor read. It was prepared to be sure
that the substructure was carefully thought out and that
all could be clearly expressed.

The detailed plan *for the introduction* came out like
this:

Introduction

1. Many of you have some acquaintance with E.
Stanley Jones—the Methodist missionary,
evangelist, and devotional writer. Stanley Jones
once spoke at the seminary, was 85.

    Had written 25 books, still going strong—
traveling, speaking, writing.

He said it was "fun being a Christian at 25, 35, 45, etc." and "it's fun being a Christian at 85 and getting funnier all the time."

2. When once asked the secret of his lifelong zest, Jones gave primary credit to two things— *grace* and *gumption*. That's quite a combination.

   (a) Grace—the undeserved mercy and power of God—God within us, loving, caring, lifting, transforming our lives. Grace and then:

   (b) Gumption—Asked daughter, "What's gumption?" Her answer: "It means rarin' to go." Gumption is personal initiative—willingness to take a task and see it through.

   (c) Grace and gumption—a great combination. The long and useful life of Stanley Jones illustrates something of what can happen when grace and gumption get together.

3. Our text gives an older example of the same combination of grace and gumption.

   a) In the last paragraph of 1st chapter Colossians Paul speaks of his purpose in life:

      to make God's word fully known: to present every person "mature in Christ"

   b) Then in v. 29 he says, "For this I toil, striving with all the energy which he mightily inspires within me."

   c) Here again grace and gumption

      (1) "For this I toil, striving"—that's gumption. Raring to go, that was Paul— traveling, preaching, writing, knocked

down and out, getting up, moving on—
that's gumption.
(2) But something more here—more basic.
Paul goes on, "For this I toil, striving *with
all the energy which* he *mightily inspires
within me.*"

An inner energy given by God—that's
not gumption, that's grace
God's own presence powerfully using
Paul's life.

d) God had the grace; and inspired by that grace,
Paul had the gumption.
(1) World hasn't been the same since.
(2) Our lives today are different because grace
and gumption got together in life of Paul
nearly 2,000 years ago.

4. We've begun thinking about E. Stanley Jones and
the Apostle Paul. What about us?
a) Can we, thinking of God's purpose for our
lives, say with Paul, "For this I toil, striving
with all the energy which he mightily inspires
within me"?
b) Can we with Stanley Jones describe our lives
as lives in which grace and gumption go
together?
c) To help answer these questions let's
(1) Take a look at four different kinds of
people. We'll call them Exhibits A, B, C,
and D.
(2) Ask ourselves as we look at each, "Is this a
picture of my life?"

(Then follows the Development beginning with Exhibit A.)

This introduction was unusually long, but this length seemed needed to tie the theme, the text, and the hearer together. The rest of the sermon was worked out in similar detail along the lines of the final rough-draft outline (pp. 108-11).

After working through the detailed outline the final step was to prepare preaching notes for the pulpit. The detailed outline could have been used, but it seemed better to prepare a set of preaching notes.

The pulpit notes for the introduction of this sermon looked as follows, including the brief pre-sermon prayer.

Prayer: Spirit of God—call us again out of ourselves into new ventures of self-forgetful trust and self-giving love. In Christ's name. Amen

Introduction
  1. Many acquainted with E. S. Jones—missionary, evangelist, etc.
     Seminary talk—85—going strong
     Fun being Christian at 25—85, funnier
  2. Secret? Grace and gumption
     a) grace—mercy—power
     b) gumption—rarin' to go—initiative
     c) quite combination—Jones illustrates
  3. Text—older example
     a) last paragraph, Col. 1—purpose—Word known—all mature

    b) last verse—*Quote v. 29*
       (1) "toil-striving"—gumption—Paul had it
       (2) more—repeat end of verse—inner energy—*grace*
    c) God had grace—Paul had gumption
       World not same—our lives different
  4. Begun with Jones and Paul—What about us?
    a) can we say v. 29 of selves?
    b) can we say grace and gumption go together in our lives?
    c) help answer—look—4 kinds—Exhibits A-B-C-D
       Ask selves of each—"Is this a picture of my life?"

These notes were written in pencil beginning at the top of the back side of a lined 9½-by-6-inch sheet which fits into a 3-ring preaching notebook. The two pages of final preaching notes looked like the example on page 116.

By going over these preaching notes a couple times on Saturday and again on Sunday morning, with the detailed outline handy for reference when needed, it was not difficult to have the basic pattern of thought and expression clearly enough in mind to be able to share it without either reading or reciting. The notes stimulated *thoughts* rather than just words. But there was no need to grope for words. Having been thought through during preparation of the detailed outline and preaching notes, wording along the lines worked out earlier naturally suggested itself. Ordered thought and alive, spontaneous expression could go together.

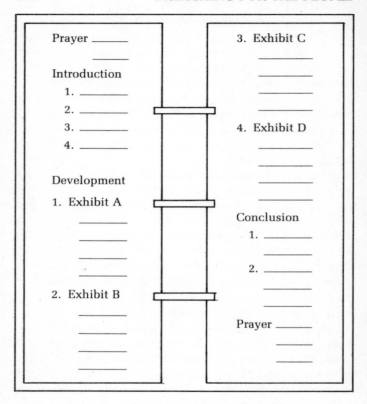

REFLECTIONS ON THE PROPOSED PROCESS

To some the process illustrated here may seem long and complex. Many sermons fall into final shape more easily than did this one. Sometimes the pattern of the first or second rough-draft outline becomes the essential plan of the final detailed outline. On other occasions it may take a half-dozen rough drafts before settling on the one to use. These rough "possible sermon plans" are often even more sketchy than those shown here. Two or three alternative plans can often be scratched out in a half hour.

There are certainly easier ways to get from text and theme to some sort of sermon. We can look over the text and then ad-lib a few pages of ramblings at the typewriter to read on Sunday morning. Or we can make a few jottings from which to ad-lib directly to the congregation. Such "methods" take less time and effort, and they certainly require less thought; but are they really worthy of "a workman who has no need to be ashamed, rightly handling the word of truth" (II Tim. 2:15)? Thinking is hard work, but is there any substitute for it? And concerning sermon preparation, is there really any substitute for some such process of gathering, selecting, and ordering thought?

Such preparation takes time and work, but in our preaching as in all of life, grace and gumption can and should go together. Indeed if we are, in any measure, to live up to the Pauline exhortation to "see that you fulfill the ministry which you have received in the Lord" (Col. 4:17), they must go together. We share Paul's ministry. Our task also is "to make the word of God fully known." We too are ministers of the "mystery hidden for ages and generations but now manifest to his saints" and are sent to proclaim Christ that we may present every person mature in him (Col. 1:25-28). Can we then do less than preach not only by grace but also with gumption? With Paul we seek to live a ministry of which we can say: "For this I toil, striving with all the energy which he mightily inspires within me" (Col. 1:29).

APPENDIX II

Questions for Personal Reflection and Group Discussion

Suggested Especially for Use in Congregational Adult Forums on Preaching and in Seminary Classes and Pastoral Seminars

On Chapter 1, "Why Should I Preach?"

(1) What kinds of sermons have been most meaningful to you? Least meaningful? Can you recall specific sermons illustrative of each?

(2) What made some sermons meaningful? What hindered the meanfulness of others?

(3) What do you hope for when you hear a sermon?

(4) Are some selfish desires sinful while others are God-given and good? Can you give examples?

(5) When is it right for the preacher to seek satisfaction of the listener's selfish desires? When is it wrong?

(6) What qualities of life do you most deeply desire? Has preaching related to these qualities? Can preaching help create these qualities?

(7) Do you think of life primarily in terms of problems to be solved or of possibilities to be fulfilled? How are these approaches to life related to each other? Is one better than the other? Why? Why not?

(8) Do you prefer that the preacher speak to your problems or to your possibilities? Or to both? What difference does it make? Can you give examples of ways preaching has helped solve your problems or fulfill your possibilities?

(9) When is "positive—possibility thinking" helpful and when is it dangerous and detrimental to Christian living?

(10) Should a preacher be motivated to preach by the call of God or by the needs of people? Or by both? What is the connection between the two?

(11) Do you believe that we are "created for Christ" and that the more fully we live in Christ the more fully human we will be? Why? Why not?

(12) Can you give examples of ways preaching has sometimes given the impression that it is sinful to be human? Is it sinful to be human? Why? Why not?

(13) Who are the most fully human persons you know or know about? What part does sin play in their lives?

(14) Do you agree that at its center Christian living consists in just two things: (1) trust in God and (2) love of people? Why? Why not? If you agree, can you say the same for true human living? Why? Why not?

(15) In what ways can we see "the soul of goodness in things evil"? To what extent is sinful living a misdirected effort to satisfy God-given desires?

(16) Why do you want your preacher to preach to you? How can you help him to address your needs more directly?

On Chapter 2, "What Should I Preach?"

(1) What has been the central message of most sermons you have heard?

(2) What message has meant the most to you? Why?

(3) What, for you, is the central message that comes to us from Jesus Christ?

(4) Can you give examples of ways in which you have heard God's yes through preaching? God's no? God's go?

(5) Has God's yes, no, or go sounded most loudly in the preaching you have heard? Which do you think we most need to hear? Why?

(6) How do you understand the distinction between preaching and teaching? Which has been predominant in sermons you have heard? Which do you think we need the most? How do they go together?

(7) How do you understand the distinction between the gospel and the law? Which have you heard most clearly in preaching? Do you agree with the "Thoughts to Ponder and Debate" (pp. 39-42)?

(8) What is the difference between being saved "by faith" and being saved "by grace through faith"? Which is the message of the gospel?

(9) Do you agree that Jesus invites us to be *passive* in trust toward God and at the same time to be *active* in love toward people? Why? Why Not?

(10) Which is the better advice to a person struggling to have faith in God: (a) "Try harder to make a decision for Christ" or (b) "Cease your struggling and trying, look and listen to Jesus Christ, and rest in the promises God gives in him"? Why?

(11) How specific should a preacher be in seeking to expose our sin and to knock the props out from under our false gods? Can you give examples of when this should be done?

(12) How specific should a preacher be in giving guidance and direction for Christian living? Can you give examples of when this should be done? Of ways it should not be done?

(13) Do we distort the gospel when we offer God's grace on certain conditions to be met? Is it correct to say, "God will love you *if* you confess, repent, and have faith?" To whom can we say, "God loves you now and will love you forever?" Do some sermons seem addressed to people whom God does not love? Is this correct? Why? Why not?

(14) What is the difference between cheap grace, conditional grace, and costly grace? Which is proclaimed in Christ? How can a preacher keep grace from seeming cheap without making it conditional? How can he keep grace from seeming conditional without making it cheap?

(15) How can a preacher who must preach Sunday after Sunday even when he does not much feel like it, keep from becoming a mechanical repeater of empty phrases? How can his hearers be of help?

(16) What do you want your preacher to preach to you? How can you help him share this message?

On Chapter 3, "How Should I Preach?"

(1) In terms of specific sermon characteristics, how

would you describe most of the preaching you have heard?

(2) What specific qualities of preaching do you appreciate the most?

(3) What specific qualities of preaching do you appreciate the least?

(4) Is it important for you that a sermon express a message of the Bible? Of a specific biblical text? Why? Why not?

(5) What is the difference between preaching about a text and preaching to fulfill the intention of a text? Which is the more biblical sermon? Why?

(6) How do you understand the distinction between pastoral and prophetic preaching? Which is most needed? How do they go together?

(7) Do you agree that some preachers speak more naturally when leading a class discussion or making announcements than in the pulpit? If this is true, what accounts for it? What can be done to help preachers be more natural in the pulpit?

(8) What effect does a preacher's thinking of words rather than thoughts have upon his communication? Upon his listener? What should be the preacher's goal in this regard? How can he best achieve it?

(9) What kind of sermon delivery do you prefer: Reading from a manuscript? Reciting from memory? Ad-libbing in the pulpit? Speaking from detailed notes? Speaking from few notes? Speaking without notes but from a plan in mind? Some other or combination of the above? What difference does it

make? What should be the preacher's goal in this regard? How can he best achieve it?

(10) What kind of sermon development do you prefer? How important is clarity? Having one central theme? Letting main points stand out? Why are these important or unimportant?

(11) Should most sermons begin with discussion about the text or with reference to the area of life addressed by the text? Why?

(12) Do you agree that careful study of the meaning and intention of a specific biblical text is the most essential part of preparation *for* a sermon? Why? Why not?

(13) Do you agree that selection and ordering of thought are the most essential parts of the preparation *of* a sermon? Why? Why not?

(14) What is the difference for speaker and hearer between inflectional emphasis imposed on content and that which rises from the preacher's alive awareness of significance of the content? Can you illustrate the difference? What should be the preacher's goal in this regard? How can he best achieve it?

(15) How do you want your preacher to preach to you? How can you help him preach more meaningfully?

(16) What steps can you take to increase partnership in preaching? Can you give feed-back and feed-in? What specific encouragement and suggestions can you share with your preacher?

NOTES

1. WHY SHOULD I PREACH?

1. See H. Grady Davis, *Design for Preaching* (Philadelphia: Fortress Press, 1958), pp. 215-17.
2. *The Preaching of F. W. Robertson*, ed. Gilbert E. Doan, Jr. (Philadelphia: Fortress Press, 1964), p. 29.
3. *The Way* (Nashville & New York: Abingdon-Cokesbury Press, 1946), p. 25.
4. Martin Luther, *Alone with God*, ed. Theodore Klienhaus (St. Louis: Concordia, 1962), p. 35.
5. *The Preaching of F. W. Robertson*, p. 161.
6. Paul Scherer, *For We Have This Treasure* (New York: Harper, 1965), p. 47.
7. Harry Emerson Fosdick, *The Living of These Days* (New York: Harper, 1956), p. 94.
8. See Norman Vincent Peale, *The Power of Positive Thinking* (Crest Books; New York: Fawcett World, 1974), and Robert Schuller, *Move Ahead with Possibility Thinking* (Garden City, N.Y.: Doubleday, 1967).

2. WHAT SHOULD I PREACH?

1. See C. H. Dodd, *The Apostolic Preaching and Its Development* (London: Hodder & Stoughton, 1949), p. 15.
2. James D. Smart, *The Teaching Ministry of the Church* (Philadelphia: Westminster Press, 1954), pp. 19, 20, 22.
3. See C. H. Spurgeon, *The Early Years 1834–1859*, "A revised edition of his autobiography originally compiled by his wife and private secretary." (London: The Banner of Truth Trust, 1962), chapter 7, "The Great Change—Conversion," pp. 79-96.
4. Paul Tillich, *The Shaking of the Foundations* (New York: Scribner's, 1953), the sermon "You Are Accepted," pp. 161-62.

5. C. F. W. Walther, *God's No and God's Yes, the Proper Distinction Between Law and Gospel,* condensed by Walter C. Pieper (St. Louis: Concordia, 1973), Thesis XIII, p. 67.
6. Scherer, *For We Have This Treasure,* p. 69.
7. Gerhard O. Forde, *Where God Meets Man, Luther's Down-to-Earth Approach to the Gospel* (Minneapolis: Augsburg, 1972), pp. 65-66.
8. See Karl Barth, *God, Grace and Gospel,* chap. 1, "Gospel and Law," pp. 3-27, trans. James Strathearn McNab, Scottish Journal of Theology Occasional Papers No. 8 (Edinburgh: Oliver & Boyd, 1959).
9. J. N. Kildahl, *The Holy Spirit and Our Faith* (former title: *Ten Studies on the Holy Spirit*) (Minneapolis: Augsburg, 1937, 1960), p. 43.
10. J. W. Stevenson, *God in My Unbelief* (New York: Harper, 1963), pp. 53-55.
11. John B. Cobb, Jr., *The Structure of Christian Existence* (Philadelphia: Westminster Press, 1967), p. 135.
12. Fosdick, *The Living of These Days,* p. 99.
13. See *The Journal of John Wesley,* as abridged by Nehemiah Curnock (New York: Capricorn Books, 1963), pp. 276, 241.
14. Leander Keck, *A Future for the Historical Jesus* (Nashville: Abingdon Press, 1971), p. 102.
15. See Dietrich Bonhoeffer, *The Cost of Discipleship,* revised and unabridged edition (New York: Macmillan, 1963), chapter 1, "Costly Grace," pp. 45-60.
16. E. Stanley Jones, *Christ and Human Suffering* (Nashville: Cokesbury Press, 1933), p. 151. See also *Selections from E. Stanley Jones* (Nashville: Abingdon Press, 1971), p. 94.
17. Kildahl, *The Holy Spirit and Our Faith,* pp. 35-36.
18. Helmut Thielicke, *The Trouble with the Church,* trans. and ed. John W. Doberstein (New York: Harper, 1965), pp. 3, 5, 6.

3. HOW SHOULD I PREACH?

1. *Ibid.,* p. 21.
2. See James Randolph, *The Renewal of Preaching* (Philadelphia: Fortress Press, 1969), "The Biblical Text in Its Intentionality," pp. 28-32.
3. Harry Emerson Fosdick, "What Is the Matter with Preaching?" *Harper's Monthly,* July 1928, p. 136.

4. See Ronald Sleeth, *Proclaiming the Gospel* (Nashville: Abingdon Press, 1964), pp. 99-104.

5. Halford E. Luccock, *In the Minister's Workshop* (Nashville & New York: Abingdon-Cokesbury Press, 1944), p. 55.

6. James A. Winans, *Speech-Making* (New York: Appleton-Century-Crofts, 1938), pp. 11-12.

7. James C. McCroskey, *An Introduction to Rhetorical Communication* (Englewood Cliffs, N.J.: Prentice-Hall, 1968), p. 213.

8. Fosdick, *The Living of These Days*, p. 95.

9. See Edmund Holt Linn, *Preaching as Counseling—The Unique Method of Harry Emerson Fosdick* (Valley Forge, Pa.: Judson Press, 1966), pp. 68-69. In this study of Fosdick's preaching, Linn uses the expression "big truth" to refer to the central message of the sermon.

10. Thielicke, *The Trouble with the Church*, p. 63.

11. See Scherer, *For We Have This Treasure*, pp. 179, 199.

12. Helmut Thielicke, *Encounter with Spurgeon*, trans. John W. Doberstein (Grand Rapids: Baker Book House, 1975), p. 40.

13. Phillips Brooks, *On Preaching* (New York: The Seabury Press, 1964), p. 152.

14. George A. Buttrick, from an unpublished sermon given as part of a "Great Preachers" series, Allentown, Pa., 1958.

15. For James Stewart's views on preaching see *Heralds of God* and *A Faith to Proclaim* (Grand Rapids: Baker Book House, reprint 1972).

16. For detailed discussion of dialogue preaching and specific examples of dialogue sermons, see William D. Thompson and Gordon C. Bennett, *Dialogue Preaching, The Shared Sermon* (Valley Forge, Pa.: Judson Press, 1969).

17. For a more complete presentation of principles and practices related to feed-back and feed-in, see Reuel L. Howe, *Partners in Preaching, Clergy and Laity in Dialogue* (New York: The Seabury Press, 1967).

APPENDIX I

1. See Reinhold Niebuhr, *The Nature and Destiny of Man*, Vol. II: *Human Destiny* (New York: Scribner's, 1943, 1964), "The Biblical Doctrine of Grace" and "Grace as Power in, and Mercy Towards, Man," pp. 100-126.